MITCHELL BEAZLEY

Photography by Jason Ingram

Lucy Bellamy

Grow5

Simple seasonal ideas for small outdoor spaces with just five plants

Lucy Bellamy

Lucy Bellamy spent five years as the editor of *Gardens Illustrated* magazine, the '*Vogue* magazine' of the gardening press. Her first book, *Brilliant and Wild*, which describes how she created a garden from scratch in a year, won the 'Practical Book of the Year' category at the 2018 Garden Media Guild awards. She has written about gardening in the national press, including for the *Guardian* and *The Times*. She lives in Bristol and has a small city garden.

Grow5

Introduction

Lucy Bellamy

The question I am asked most regularly is: 'What can I plant in my garden?' This is often followed by the description of a tiny outdoor space. With so many wonderful plants to choose from, it can be difficult to choose the best ones for your plot.

In my work, I am lucky to be able to visit inspiring gardens in the UK and internationally, and to call upon leading garden designers, gardeners and nursery people, cherry-picking ideas. As the owner of a small city garden in the middle of Bristol, southwest England, I want a space that's everchanging, thrums with colour and scent, and hums with bees and butterflies; somewhere I can hang out at the end of each day with my little dog, Reg.

Grow5 is based on a few simple premises: how to choose plants, how to combine them, and why they work well together. Why five? Using five plants draws on a key design principle: repetition. A combination of five allows the plants to provide the excitement in a garden and perform the heavy lifting of the design work. Five works to nature's rules, where it's rare to see just one of any plant growing. Think of a woodland floor in early spring woven with celandine, wood anemone, primroses, sweet violets and grasses or mixed moorland grasses spotted with harebells and orchids - both use repeating palettes of only a few plants.

From an urban garden inspired by an ancient hedgerow, to a micro meadow in a city space, to a riff on an English flower garden, this book contains 52 ideas, using only five plants each and suitable for every type of small outdoor space.

'A combination of five allows the plants to provide the excitement in a garden and perform the heavy lifting of the design work.'

The rounded shape, heavy lip and rusty patination give this cast-iron pot a utilitarian feel which juxtaposes well with the pretty, tiny plants. The combination is reminiscent of a forest floor in springtime. Vita Sackville-West, who created the garden at Sissinghurst, in Kent, England, likened planting in pots to a jeweller working with precious stones - there is something very appealing about cultivating a collection of miniature things.

The key plant here, *Pulmonaria* OPAL ('Ocupol'), has speckled leaves and pale blue flowers. Like other pulmonaria cultivars, it has flowering stamina and is a good choice for a shaded situation, offering luminosity even on gloomier days. The *Anemone blanda* will also glow in limited light. *Galanthus nivalis*, *Scilla siberica* and *Muscari armeniacum,* three of the very earliest flowering bulbs, push up to flower between the two main plants.

Method

1 Choose a good-sized pot and drill drainage holes in the base, if there aren't some already. Position the pot first, as it will be difficult to move once filled with compost. Fill the pot a quarter full with horticultural grit to encourage water to drain freely.

2 Plants in pots are reliant on what you provide for them, so use a good-quality compost. A peat-free, general-purpose compost with a few scoops of grit is ideal. Fill the pot with the gritty compost, leaving a centimetre (half an inch) or so between the top of the compost and the rim to provide space for watering.

3 Plant the *Pulmonaria* OPAL ('Ocupol') first to provide the base note. Tap each plant out of its pot and gently loosen a few of the roots with your fingertips. Dig a hole for each plant to the same depth it was in its pot, then plant and firm in gently with your hands. Repeat this process with the *Anemone blanda.*

4 Add the *Galanthus nivalis, Muscari armeniacum* and *Scilla siberica,* gently pushing them out of their pots from the underside and keeping as much compost around the roots as possible. Scoop out holes, plant and firm in. Add more compost to fill any gaps between the plants and then use a layer of gravel to cover the compost to stop the plants getting splashed when it rains. Water thoroughly.

5 If you wish to grow the *Galanthus* and *Muscari* from bulbs first, plant three of each in small, individual pots in autumn ready to transfer to the main pot when they bud. Plant the snowdrops a few weeks later than the *Muscari*, otherwise they can skip ahead.

The 5 plants

1

Anemone blanda

2

Galanthus nivalis

3

Muscari armeniacum

4

Pulmonaria OPAL ('Ocupol')

5

Scilla siberica

3

Muscari armeniacum
grape hyacinth

Ink-blue bobbles sit above green, strap-shaped leaves.

bulb
height 20cm (8in)
5 per pot
flowers from late winter to early spring

2

Galanthus nivalis
snowdrop

Very much the bulb of pre-spring. Dipped, white flowers with green markings on the inner petals.

bulb
height 15cm (6in)
3 per pot
flowers from mid-winter to early spring

1

Anemone blanda
winter windflower

Bright violet flowers with narrow petals and yellow centres. The undersides of the leaves have a pink tone.

perennial
height 80cm (32in)
1 per pot
flowers from late winter to mid-spring

4

Pulmonaria
Opal ('Ocupol')
lungwort

Sky-blue flowers
and speckled
leaves. A very
useful plant for a
gloomier position.

perennial
height 20cm (8in)
3 per pot
*flowers from
late winter to
early spring*

5

Scilla siberica
Siberian squill

Tiny, star-like flowers in lapis-lazuli
blue tinged with white.

bulb
height 20cm (8in)
5 per pot
flowers from late winter to mid-spring

Good for...

early bumblebee queens
bumblebees
solitary bees (including the
hairy-footed flower bee)
hoverflies

There is great pleasure to be found in spending a few hours mixing and matching small plants with small pots. This collection for a tabletop singles out small plants that might otherwise be dwarfed outside and pairs them with suitable containers, bearing their colours and habits in mind. The beauty of a collection such as this is that as one plant goes over, it can be easily swapped for something else just coming into flower.

This display includes three alpine plants and two bulbs - all plants that don't need a long root run and so are up to the challenge of growing in a small vessel. In the wild, alpines grow in rocky crevices with a tendency to dry out suddenly and completely, which makes them a good choice for small containers, while *Crocus* 'Ruby Giant' and *Fritillaria meleagris* are both small bulbs that flower early, when there are few resources about.

I chose an eclectic group of taller and shorter vessels, which I picked up as and when I saw them, to reflect the habits of the plants they hold. Reclamation yards and junk shops are good sources of small, stylish pots, but you can use any container that has, or has the potential to have, a drainage hole made in the base. Upright, angular *Fritillaria meleagris* benefits from the space of a wide, open pan to show off its geometry to good effect, while a shallow, scallop-edged tin that I picked up for a few euros while travelling is a good match for *Viola labradorica*'s hump of round, dark leaves - I like the way the viola doesn't completely fill the pot. The simple curve of a brown clay pot emphasizes the mossy bump of *Saxifraga* × *arendsii* 'Buttercream' beautifully.

Method

1 Gather together the plants and start matching them to your assortment of pots, taking into consideration the individual character, colour and habit of each plant. Give some thought to how the pots work together as a group too, and whether you want them to match or mismatch. Drill some drainage holes in the bases of the pots, if there aren't some already.

2 Cover the hole in each pot with a pebble to keep the compost inside and pour in a generous layer of horticultural grit to encourage water to drain freely.

3 Partially fill each container with equal measures of peat-free, general-purpose compost and grit to make a beautifully open mix.

4 Tap each plant out of its pot, keeping as much of the compost around the roots as possible, and plant it in your choice of container. Use your fingers to push a little more compost around the sides to fill any gaps.

5 Add a layer of gravel to cover the surface of the compost to stop the plants getting splashed when it rains. Water the pots gently.

6 Stand the containers on an outdoor table, ideally somewhere they will avoid too much winter wet.

Note: This display would work equally well arranged on a doorstep.

The 5 plants

1

Crocus 'Ruby Giant'

2

Fritillaria meleagris

3

Saxifraga × *arendsii* 'Buttercream'

4

Veronica umbrosa 'Georgia Blue'

5

Viola labradorica

1

Crocus
'Ruby Giant'
crocus

Orange anthers
(like the Pantone
Colour Clockwork
Orange) and proper
purple flowers.
Each strap-like leaf
has a white stripe
down the middle.

bulb
height 10cm (4in)
5 per pot
*flowers from
late winter to
early spring*

2

Fritillaria meleagris
snake's head fritillary

Nodding, blackcurrant and white flowers
patterned like a chequered flag. The
common name - snake's head fritillary -
refers to the reptilian-looking flower buds.

bulb
height 30cm (12in)
6 per pot
flowers from mid-spring to late spring

3

Saxifraga
× *arendsii*
'Buttercream'
mossy saxifrage

Clumps of dark
green, moss-like
foliage and flowers
that resemble small,
milk-white stars.

perennial
height 15cm (6in)
1 per pot
*flowers from early
spring to late spring*

4

Veronica umbrosa 'Georgia Blue'
speedwell

Electric-blue flowers at the tips of
pleasingly gangly stems.

perennial
height 20cm (8in)
1 per pot
flowers from early spring to early summer

5

*Viola
labradorica*
Labrador violet

Dark, scalloped
leaves and
miniature, violet-
coloured flowers.

perennial
height 20cm (8in)
1 per pot
*flowers from
early spring to
mid-autumn*

Good for...

early bumblebee queens
honeybees
solitary bees
hoverflies

In spring I like to plant a pot of early risers. These delicate but robust little plants are best enjoyed at close quarters, so you can fully appreciate how beautiful they are. This clay bowl includes two evergreens - a fern and an *Epimedium* - and three different bulbs in a palette of plum, green and white.

I usually plant the bulbs in small, individual pots in the preceding autumn, three of each cultivar to a pot, ready for transferring to the main container with the evergreens in late winter, but it is also possible to buy them as pots of budding bulbs in early spring. A clay pot looks stylish and it is also a good practical choice for bulbs, as its porosity means that they are never sitting in overly wet compost.

Method

1   Gather together all the plants. Choose a wide clay pot that isn't too deep. Cover the hole in the base of the pot with a pebble to keep the compost inside and pour in a generous layer of horticultural grit to ensure sharp drainage.

2   It's important to use a good-quality compost as plants growing in pots are completely reliant on what you provide for them. Fill the pot with a peat-free, general-purpose compost and add a few scoops of grit, leaving a centimetre (half an inch) or so between the top of the compost and the rim for watering.

3   First, plant the *Polystichum polyblepharum* as a base layer. Scoop out a hole in the compost towards the edge of the pot. Tap the fern out of its pot and gently loosen a few of the roots with your fingertips. Plant the fern to the same depth it was in its pot and carefully firm in. Repeat this planting process for the *Epimedium*.

4   Next, add the flowering bulbs - *Fritillaria melagris, F. michailovskyi* and *Narcissus* 'Tresamble' - pushing them out of their pots from the underside if they are tricky to free. Keep as much of the compost around the bulbs as possible and take care not to damage the flower stalks, which can be quite brittle and easy to snap. Scoop out a hole for each bulb, plant and firm in.

5   Tuck some extra compost in between each of the plants to fill any gaps, using your fingers to push it down.

6   Using a handful of gravel to cover the compost will link the plants visually and stop the smallest flowers getting splashed when it rains. Water thoroughly.

The 5 plants

1

Epimedium pinnatum subsp. *colchicum*

2

Fritillaria meleagris

3

Fritillaria michailovskyi

4

Narcissus 'Tresamble'

5

Polystichum polyblepharum

1

Epimedium pinnatum
subsp. *colchicum*
Colchian barrenwort

Panicles of citrus-lemon flowers and
plum-toned foliage. Evergreen.

perennial
height 30cm (12in)
1 per pot
flowers from early spring to mid-spring

3

*Fritillaria
michailovskyi*
**Michailovski
fritillary**

Grey-green leaves
and plum flowers
with yellow tips.
Honey scent.

bulb
height 15cm (6in)
6 per pot
*flowers from
mid-spring to
late spring*

2

Fritillaria meleagris
snake's head fritillary

A small bulb with nodding, plum and white
flowers that are patterned like a chequered
flag. The common name refers to the flower
buds, which look like a snake's head.

bulb
height 30cm (12in)
6 per pot
flowers from mid-spring to late spring

4

Narcissus 'Tresamble'
daffodil

Milk-white, sweptback petals. The buds
dip pleasingly just before the flowers open.
A heritage daffodil that dates from the
1930s. Honey scent.

bulb
height 30cm (12in)
6 per pot
flowers from early spring to mid-spring

5

*Polystichum
polyblepharum*
tassel fern

Evergreen fern with
fresh new fronds
that unfurl each
spring and look like
a shuttlecock.

perennial
height 80cm (32in)
1 per pot
evergreen foliage

Good for...

early bumblebee queens
honeybees
solitary bees
hoverflies
bee-flies

Pale blue is best used in the shadows where it glows and appears to hover. This pot combines a beautifully arching *Polygonatum × hybridum* with low, green filler plants, including *Pulmonaria* OPAL ('Ocupol') with pale blue flowers, which all enjoy shady conditions. *Polygonatum × hybridum* hints at the woodland edge, gently bobbing in the breeze and adding height with its small, dangling flowers. I've used three different species of fern, but you could use more or fewer, depending on the size of your pot. The light-reflecting, silvery leaves of *Athyrium niponicum* var. *pictum* are ideal in dappled conditions and I particularly like the wide-toothed fronds of the *Arachnoides aristata* 'Variegata'. The colour and patination of this cast-iron pot suggest a depth of dark, moist, humus-rich soil, the same conditions that all these plants favour.

The 5 plants

Method

1 Choose a big pot and drill some drainage holes in the base if there aren't some already. Cover the holes in the base of the pot with a pebble to keep the compost inside.

2 These plants all like cool, moisture-retentive, yet well-drained conditions. Fill the pot with peat-free, general-purpose compost and leave a centimetre (half an inch) or so between the top of the compost and the rim for watering.

3 Arrange the plants in the large pot, keeping them in their pots to begin with. This composition relies on form and texture, so spend some time getting the placement right. Start with the three *Pulmonaria* OPAL ('Ocupol'), spacing the plants out evenly.

4 Next, add the *Athyrium niponicum* var. *pictum* and *Arachnoides aristata* 'Variegata' in between the pulmonarias, spacing them so they will thread together when they grow.

5 Tuck in the two *Polystichum tsussimense* to fill the gaps. This is a relatively slow-growing fern, so you can pack them in quite snugly.

6 Finally, add the *Polygonatum × hybridum*, planting them towards the edges of the pot so that they will arch inwards.

7 When you are happy with the composition, push the ferns out of their pots from the underside, as they are likely to be firmly rooted. Use a sharp tap on a firm surface to ease the *Pulmonaria* and *Polygonatum* from their pots. Loosen a few of the roots of each plant to encourage them to grow outwards into the compost before scooping out the holes and planting them at the same depth they were in their pots.

8 Firm the plants in gently using your hands and, if necessary, tuck some extra compost in between them to fill any gaps. Water thoroughly.

Note: This combination of ferns and perennials will repeat each spring.

1
Arachnoides aristata 'Variegata'

2
Athyrium niponicum var. *pictum*

3
Polygonatum × hybridum

4
Polystichum tsussimense

5
Pulmonaria OPAL ('Ocupol')

3

Polygonatum × hybridum
Solomon's seal

Dangling, white flowers, tinged with green at the tips, on graceful, arching stems. Indispensable for a shaded garden.

perennial
height 80cm (32in)
2 per pot
flowers from mid-spring to early summer

2

Athyrium niponicum var. *pictum*
painted lady fern

Deciduous fern with plum-coloured stems and soft grey fronds with a metallic sheen.

perennial
height 30cm (12in)
1 per pot
new green fronds unfurl each spring

1

Arachnoides aristata 'Variegata'
East Indian holly fern

A deciduous fern that has fresh, green fronds with lemon midribs.

perennial
height 30cm (12in)
1 per pot
new green fronds unfurl each spring

4

Polystichum tsussimense
Korean rock fern

A small, evergreen fern which is tufted with fresh, bright green fronds.

perennial
height 45cm (18in)
2 per pot
evergreen foliage

5

Pulmonaria OPAL ('Ocupol')
lungwort

Spotty leaves and sky-blue flowers that look luminous in gloomy conditions.

perennial
height 20cm (8in)
3 per pot
flowers from late winter to early spring

Good for...

early bumblebee queens
bumblebees
solitary bees
hoverflies

The cool, green palette of this courtyard suggests a woodland edge where early-flowering opportunists make the most of a window of light before the tree canopy above them comes into leaf. This combination is a good choice for a partially shady garden with shadows cast by overhanging trees, either from within the garden or from over the wall or fence. The *Euphorbia griffithii* and *Dodecatheon jeffreyi* offer pools of colour among the textural greens of *Sesleria autumnalis* grasses, while *Euphorbia griffithii*'s resilient nature and orange-peel flowers make it indispensable for a challenging spot. *Allium tripedale*, used here as a dot plant, has a good number of clear pink and white flowers and is more heavily flowered than its commonly planted cousin *Allium siculum,* which could be used as an alternative. *Lilium martagon* is a beautiful and hardworking lily that is especially useful in a small space and has the benefit of offering good foliage in spring ahead of its late-summer flowers.

The 5 plants

1

Allium tripedale

Method

1 Use a spade to dig over the soil to a crumbly consistency, breaking up any big lumps.

2 Gather together all the plants.

3 Starting with the *Sesleria autumnalis*, space the plants out on the soil, still in their pots. This is a low-growing, clump-forming grass, so position the plants fairly close together, creating groups of two or three, leaving a gap and then repeating this nearby.

4 Add the *Dodecatheon jeffreyi* in one or two bigger groups, and include the occasional single-plant outlier.

5 Dot the *Euphorbia griffithii* 'Dixter' in between the *Sesleria* so that the vibrant stems and flowers will stand out against the green background. Repeat this with the *Lilium martagon* and *Allium tripedale*.

6 Review the composition, looking for ups and downs - you are aiming for taller plants that jump up next to others which are low and quiet.

7 Tap each plant out of its pot and loosen a few of the roots with your fingertips. Dig a hole for each plant to the same depth it was in its pot before planting and firming the soil down gently with your hands. Water all the plants thoroughly.

8 If you'd like to grow the bulbs from scratch, plant the *Allium tripedale* in autumn and the *Lilium martagon* in late winter to flower the following year. Dig holes, 10-15cm (4-6in) deep, and bury each of the bulbs with the pointy end facing upwards.

2

Dodecatheon jeffreyi

3

Euphorbia griffithii 'Dixter'

4

Lilium martagon

5

Sesleria autumnalis

2

Dodecatheon jeffreyi
Sierra shooting star

Pale pink flowers
with sharply
reflexed petals
and pointed tips.

perennial
height 30cm (12in)
3 per m² (10ft²)
*flowers from early
spring to late spring*

1

Allium tripedale
honey garlic

Pale pink and white flowers that are
large enough for a bumblebee to crawl
inside. After pollination, the flowers turn
upwards to form pointed seedheads.
Reliably perennial.

bulb
height 90cm (36in)
2 per m² (10ft²)
flowers from mid-spring to late summer

3

Euphorbia griffithii 'Dixter'
spurge

Crimson stems, bronze-tinged foliage
and citrus-orange flowers.

perennial
height 80cm (32in)
1 per m² (10ft²)
flowers from early summer to early autumn

5

Sesleria autumnalis
autumn moor grass

Bright green, evergreen grass in wiry
clumps with fleeting tufts of pale flowers.

grass
height 1.2m (4ft)
5 per m² (10ft²)
flowers from early summer to mid-autumn

4

Lilium martagon
Turk's cap lily

Whorls of dark green leaves in spring and
crimson-speckled, pink flowers in summer.

bulb
height 75cm (30in)
1 per m² (10ft²)
flowers from early summer to mid-summer

Good for...

bumblebees
solitary bees
hoverflies
ladybirds

I like the simplicity of bulbs: papery packages that contain everything needed to grow into a fully fledged flowers. Tulips are the obvious choice in spring and this planting scheme by garden designer Tom Stuart-Smith uses them in good numbers. Spring bulbs require some forethought as the bulbs must be planted in the previous autumn to spend winter underground in the cold and dark. The drop in temperature allows the bud to develop inside the bulb and stimulates a plant hormone, gibberellin, which pulls the leaves and stem up to the light when the time is right.

Planting the bulbs in pools of each colour gives the display a contemporary feel, even when the colours are pick-and-mix. Here, tulips in plum, orange and blackcurrant are layered like a trifle, with *Narcissus* 'Thalia' and *N.* 'Toto' providing a muted note.

Method

1 **In autumn** Use a spade to dig over the soil to a crumbly consistency, breaking up any big lumps.

2 Dig an individual hole for each bulb, 15cm (6in) deep, and bury them with their pointy ends facing upwards.

3 Cover the bulbs with soil and tamp down with your hands.

The 5 plants

1
Narcissus 'Thalia'

2
Narcissus 'Toto'

3
Tulipa 'Ballerina'

4
Tulipa 'Merlot'

5
Tulipa 'Rems Favourite'

1

Narcissus 'Thalia'
daffodil

A very early-flowering daffodil. Ivory-white flowers with a subtle vanilla scent.

bulb
height 45cm (18in)
20 per m² (10ft²)
flowers from early spring to mid-spring

2

Narcissus 'Toto'
daffodil

A miniature daffodil with three pale, star-shaped flowers atop each stalk. Vanilla scent.

bulb
height 20cm (8in)
20 per m² (10ft²)
flowers from early spring to mid-spring

3

Tulipa 'Ballerina'
tulip

A lily-flowered tulip with pointed petal tips; the striking orange colour intensifies as the flower ages.

bulb
height 40cm (16in)
15 per m² (10ft²)
flowers from mid-spring to late spring

5

Tulipa 'Rems Favourite'
tulip

Egg-shaped flowers swirled with
the colours of a blackcurrant fool.

bulb
height 40cm (16in)
15 per m² (10ft²)
flowers from mid-spring to late spring

4

Tulipa 'Merlot'
tulip

A purple, lily-flowered tulip with
pointed petal tips.

bulb
height 50cm (20in)
15 per m² (10ft²)
flowers from mid-spring to late spring

Good for...

early bumblebee queens
bumblebees
solitary bees

I was living in a rented flat in Bristol, England, when I first visited Hillside, the private garden of designer Dan Pearson. Dan's work is as exciting as it is varied, from the achingly cool London courtyard garden he designed for *Vogue* fashion photographer Juergen Teller to a woodland flora garden on the Japanese island of Hokkaido that is said to be sustainable for 1,000 years. Dan shares what he is planting at Hillside on *Dig Delve*, an online magazine, where he notes the details of his tulip trials each year. New tulips are carefully selected according to colour, but are then thrown together at random so their colours and forms juxtapose and collide.

As most tulips flower reliably only once, they are a good choice for renters. This pot uses a palette of sloe-purple, scarlet and cardinal red, as well as flowers with varied shapes, all inspired by Hillside. Tulip bulbs need to be planted in late autumn so they can spend winter under the soil in the cold and dark. Low temperatures allow the flower buds to develop inside the bulbs, so that they are ready to push up into the warmth and light the following spring.

Method

1 **In autumn** Choose as big a pot as you can find and drill some drainage holes in the base, if there aren't some already. Cover the holes with a pebble to keep the compost inside. Fill the pot with peat-free, general-purpose compost, making sure you leave a centimetre (half an inch) or so between the compost and the rim for watering.

2 Tip the bulbs out of their bags onto a sheet of newspaper and mix them up thoroughly using your hands.

3 Scatter the bulbs on the surface of the compost, spacing them so they are at least one finger's width apart and with the pointy ends facing upwards.

4 Bury the bulbs in the compost to a depth of 15cm (6in), making a hole for each one and dropping it in. Carefully cover the bulbs with more compost and gently tamp down the surface.

5 Water the bulbs thoroughly to give them a good start in the container.

Note: These tulips will last a good six weeks from the first flower to the last.

The 5 plants

1

Tulipa 'Continental'

2

Tulipa 'Merlot'

3

Tulipa 'National Velvet'

4

Tulipa 'Palmyra'

5

Tulipa 'Victoria's Secret'

1

Tulipa
'Continental'
tulip

One of the darkest
tulips available.
Egg-shaped flowers
with deep plum-
coloured petals.

bulb
height 45cm (18in)
10 per pot
*flowers from mid-
spring to late spring*

2

Tulipa 'Merlot'
tulip

A purple, lily-flowered tulip with pointed petals.

bulb
height 50cm (20in)
10 per pot
flowers from mid-spring to late spring

3

Tulipa
'National Velvet'
tulip

Strawberry-jam
red and slightly
iridescent, egg-
shaped flowers.

bulb
height 50cm (20in)
10 per pot
*flowers from mid-
spring to late spring*

4

Tulipa 'Palmyra'
tulip

A double tulip with damson-coloured flowers. Blooms early for a double tulip.

bulb
height 30cm (12in)
10 per pot
flowers from mid-spring to late spring

5

Tulipa 'Victoria's Secret'
tulip

Undulating petals that twist and turn. Deep rose-pink.

bulb
height 50cm (20in)
10 per pot
flowers from mid-spring to late spring

Good for...

early bumblebee queens
bumblebees
solitary bees

Nature has a way of effortlessly arranging itself into beautiful and harmonious patterns. This late-spring plan adopts a pointillist approach, with points of colour working together to create bolder shapes. *Allium* 'Miami', *Cirsium rivulare* 'Atropurpureum' and the tall grass, *Stipa gigantea*, all have flower heads made up of lots of minute flowers. The fennel leaves provide a background foil for the bulbs and perennials, while *Iris* 'Sable' in rock-and-roll purple roves gently through. This meadow-esque design feels unexpected in a small city garden and has even more impact as a result. In summer the fennel has yellow flowers.

Method

1 Use a spade to dig over the soil to a crumbly consistency, breaking up any big lumps.

2 Gather together all the plants.

3 Starting with the *Stipa gigantea*, space the plants out on the soil, still in their pots. This is a tall, airy plant, so consider how it will look in different spots, including when you view the scheme through the windows of your home.

4 Add the *Cirsium rivulare* 'Atropurpureum' and *Foeniculum vulgare*, in ones and twos, so that the flowers and foliage mingle at the tips.

5 Dot the *Iris* 'Sable' at random among the other plants. Make sure not to place them too close together as they will grow to be quite hefty plants.

6 When every plant has a spot, dig a hole for the *Stipa*, *Cirsium* and *Foeniculum*. Tap each plant from its pot and winkle out a few of the roots using your fingertips. Dig a hole for each plant to the same depth it was in its pot before planting and firming the soil down gently with your hands.

7 Next, plant the irises. Take care not to plant them too deeply, as the top of the rhizome (the woody stem that looks like a root) needs to stay above the soil. Water thoroughly.

8 Alliums are best planted as dormant bulbs in the preceding autumn. Bury the bulbs, 10-15cm (4-6in) deep, with their pointy ends facing upwards, tucking them between the other flowers. You can also buy them as budding bulbs in early summer, if you prefer.

Note: The flowers in this display shed their petals discreetly, which is useful in a small space.

The 5 plants

1
Allium 'Miami'

2
Cirsium rivulare 'Atropurpureum'

3
Foeniculum vulgare

4
Iris 'Sable'

5
Stipa gigantea

1

Allium 'Miami'
ornamental onion

Geometric spheres of violet flowers that are good for bees. Architectural seedheads in winter.

bulb
height 80cm (32in)
5 per m² (10ft²)
flowers from late spring to early summer

2

Cirsium rivulare 'Atropurpureum'
plume thistle

A colourful cultivated form of the wild thistle, with jagged, dark green leaves and toasted-pink flowers.

perennial
height 1.5m (5ft)
1 per m² (10ft²)
flowers from early summer to early autumn

3

Foeniculum vulgare
fennel

Feathery, bright green foliage and chartreuse, umbel flowers. Edible, from root to flower.

perennial
height 1.8m (6ft)
2 per m² (10ft²)
flowers from mid-summer to late summer

4

Iris 'Sable'
bearded iris

A scented iris in vibrant purple. Elegant and not too big.

perennial
height 90cm (36in)
1 per m² (10ft²)
flowers from late spring to early summer

5

Stipa gigantea
golden oats

Ribbon leaves and tiny, papery flowers on stems 2m (6½ft) tall. The delicate seedheads last all winter. Semi-evergreen.

grass
height 2m (6½ft)
1 per m² (10ft²)
flowers from early summer to mid-summer

Good for...

bumblebees
solitary bees
hoverflies
butterflies
damsel bugs
shield bugs
ladybirds
hibernating lacewing larvae

Urban soils are typically quite hungry for nutrients, but lots of plants grow better in such 'scratchy' soil. There may even be rubble in your soil if you live in a newly built house or building work has taken place nearby. A gravel garden emphasizes the lines and textures of the plants rather than their colours, and the sense of space also comes into play. Planting in gravel makes plants look wispier and more angular with sharper outlines, but also physically robust; they flower for longer and there is less recourse to the watering can. Here, layers of flowers with gently repeating shapes make the most of a small space. *Allium atropurpureum*, a more solid flower, picks up the outline of *Ammi majus,* which is light and airy. This vertical stalk/round top combination is echoed in the soft nubs of *Salvia argentea* 'Artemis' buds. Colour is minimal, but given some space, all the plants can catch the light.

The 5 plants

Method

1 Use locally sourced gravel if you can; with fewer 'gravel' miles involved, this is a better environmental choice.

2 Gravel should be 5-10cm (2-4in) deep for planting in. Buy enough gravel to cover any bare soil, thinking about where the gravel will start and end - perhaps butting against a wall or tamped down at the edge to become a path.

3 Tip the gravel straight onto the soil from the bag. The worms will pull some of the stones down into the soil, which is a good thing because this will increase drainage further.

4 Gather together all the plants and, keeping them in their original pots, water the compost thoroughly.

5 Space the plants out on the gravel, arranging them thoughtfully so you have different-sized spaces between them. Aim for a series of ups and downs, keeping the eventual heights of the plants in mind.

6 To plant, tap each plant out if its pot, retaining a little of the compost around the roots. Scoop out a hole in the gravel and soil using your hands, put the plant in and nudge the gravel back into place, right up to the stem. Water all the plants once more.

1

Allium atropurpureum

2

Ammi majus

3

Hylotelephium 'Matrona'

4

Lychnis floscuculi 'Nana'

5

Salvia argentea 'Artemis'

1

Allium
atropurpureum
ornamental onion

Starburst flowers that are the colour
of blackcurrant cordial. In winter, the
seedheads echo the shape of the flowers.

bulb
height 75cm (30in)
8 per m² (10ft²)
flowers from late spring to early summer

2

Ammi majus
bishop's flower

Like an airy cow
parsley with tall,
almost leafless
stems and white,
umbel flowers. Very
popular with bees.

annual
height 1.2m (4ft)
1 per m² (10ft²)
*flowers from
early summer to
early autumn*

3

Hylotelephium 'Matrona'
stonecrop

Chunky corymb flowers and waxy leaves.
Architectural seedheads in winter, that last.

perennial
height 70cm (28in)
2 per m² (10ft²)
flowers from late summer to mid-autumn

5

Salvia argentea 'Artemis'
silver sage

Big, felty leaves and buds that open in summer to milk-yellow flowers.

perennial
height 90cm (36in)
3 per m² (10ft²)
flowers from mid-summer to late summer

4

Lychnis floscuculi 'Nana'
dwarf ragged robin

Small, ragged flowers in brilliant pink. *Lychnis* is also straightforward to grow from seed, if you wish.

perennial
height 15cm (6in)
2 per m² (10ft²)
flowers from spring to early summer

Good for...

bumblebees
solitary bees
small beetles
hoverflies
butterflies
moths
hibernating solitary bees, ladybirds and lacewings and their larvae

Garden designer Piet Oudolf is the founding father of the New Perennial Movement, a way of designing with plants that celebrates them at every stage in their lifecycle. Instead of cutting back spent flowers when they fade, blooms are left in situ, evolving into architectural seedheads that last throughout the colder months. The film *Five Seasons: The Gardens of Piet Oudolf*, directed by Thomas Piper, delineates the Oudolf Field, a garden/living art installation at Hauser & Wirth Somerset, through five consecutive stages, from bud to flower to seedhead to bud and into flower again. A garden that works in every season is especially important in a small space where even during the colder months the plants can all be seen through the windows of the home. *Allium christophii, A. siculum, Rudbeckia occidentalis* and *Salvia × sylvestris* 'Rose Queen' are washed with colour from spring into summer. In autumn and winter their resilient seedheads echo the shapes of the preceding flowers.

The 5 plants

1

Allium christophii

2

Allium siculum

Method

1 **In autumn** Use a spade to dig over the soil to a crumbly consistency, breaking up any big lumps.

2 Scatter the *Allium christophii* and *A. siculum* bulbs randomly on the soil.

3 Dig a hole for each bulb, 15cm (6in) deep, and drop it inside with the pointy end facing upwards. Cover the bulbs with soil and tamp down.

4 **In spring** Gather together the *Geranium* 'Orion', *Rudbeckia occidentalis* and *Salvia × sylvestris* 'Rose Queen'.

5 Thinking of each plant as a member of a group rather than an individual, space the plants out on the soil, still in their pots, in an undulating pattern. Position one plant and then another nearby, allowing the two plants to come together at their tips.

6 Tap each plant from its pot and ease the roots out a little with your fingertips. Dig a hole for each plant to the same depth it was in its pot before planting and firming in gently with your hands. Water all the plants thoroughly.

Note: When new green shoots push up though the soil in spring, use a pair of secateurs to cut all the plants back to soil level ready to repeat the flowering cycle.

3

Geranium 'Orion'

4

Rudbeckia occidentalis

5

Salvia × sylvestris 'Rose Queen'

3

Geranium
'Orion'
**cranesbill,
hardy geranium**

Prussian-blue
flowers and lots of
leafy foliage. Darker
lines on the insides
of the petals act as
street markings for
pollinators, guiding
them to the nectar
and pollen inside.

perennial
height 40cm (16in)
2 per m² (10ft²)
*flowers from
late spring to
early autumn*

2

Allium siculum
Sicilian honey garlic

Green-white flowers tinged with plum-pink.
The waxy, individual florets are big enough
for a large bumblebee to crawl completely
inside. After the flowers have been
pollinated, they point sharply upwards.

bulb
height 1.2m (4ft)
5 per m² (10ft²)
flowers from late spring to early summer

1

Allium christophii
star of Persia

Violet, starburst flowers atop straight
stems. The winter seedheads repeat the
starburst shape of the flowers.

bulb
height 60cm (24in)
4 per m² (10ft²)
flowers from late spring to early summer

4

Rudbeckia occidentalis
western coneflower

Striking, black bobble flowers on tall stems. Black bobble seedheads follow in winter.

perennial
height 1.5m (5ft)
2 per m² (10ft²)
flowers from early summer to late summer

5

Salvia × sylvestris 'Rose Queen'
wood sage

Vertical spikes of small, rose-pink, trumpet-like flowers.

perennial
height 60cm (24in)
3 per m² (10ft²)
flowers from early summer to mid-autumn

Good for...

bumblebees
solitary bees
hoverflies
butterflies
winter homes in hollow stems for hibernating solitary bees and ladybirds

This small, shady garden is imbued with the mood of a woodland glade. Height is vital in a small space, and in this 'pocket planting' ferns and the pretty, light-reflecting grass *Melica altissima* 'Alba' are speared by the stems of the skyward-reaching foxglove, *Digitalis lutea*. In their natural environment foxgloves are pioneers, happy to lie dormant when the woodland canopy is too dense, but the first to respond to a gap in the foliage and a window of light. Unusually for a foxglove, *D. lutea* is reliably perennial and has small, dainty flowers. Useful in early summer for its emergent foliage, *Thalictrum delavayi* 'Album' has white flowers a metre (39 inches) high in summer, when the foxgloves have finished for the year.

The 5 plants

1
Digitalis lutea

2
Dryopteris erythrosora

3
Hakonechloa macra

4
Melica altissima 'Alba'

5
Thalictrum delavayi 'Album'

Method

1 Use a spade to dig over the soil to a crumbly consistency, breaking up any big lumps. The plants used here are woodland dwellers that like a cool, moisture-retentive soil and will appreciate a few spadefuls of good-quality, peat-free, general-purpose compost added to the planting hole.

2 Gather all the plants together.

3 Starting with the *Hakonechloa macra*, *Melica altissima* 'Alba' and *Thalictrum delavayi* 'Album', arrange the plants in their pots on the soil in a loose, tessellating pattern.

4 Add the *Digitalis lutea* asymmetrically within the composition and towards the back.

5 Tuck the ferns in at the edge, allowing the unfurling fronds to overhang the path or edge of the border.

6 Remove the plants from their pots and loosen a few of the roots with your fingertips. If the ferns are firmly rooted in their pots, push them out from the underside. Dig a hole for each plant to the same depth it was in its pot, then plant and firm down the soil gently using your hands. Water all the plants thoroughly.

1

Digitalis lutea
small yellow foxglove

Delicate spires of small, primrose-yellow flowers. Popular with bees. A reliably perennial foxglove.

perennial
height 60cm (24in)
1 per m² (10ft²)
flowers from late spring to mid-summer

2

Dryopteris erythrosora
copper shield fern

Feathery, bright green foliage with a black midrib. Fresh new fronds with a copper hue unfurl each spring. Deciduous.

perennial
height 75cm (30in)
1 per m² (10ft²)
new green fronds unfurl each spring

3

Hakonechloa macra
Japanese forest grass

A graceful, decidous grass with arching, overlapping leaves. Very slow growing.

grass
height 30cm (12in)
3 per m² (10ft²)
flowers from late summer to early autumn, but usually grown for its foliage

5

Thalictrum delavayi 'Album'
meadow rue

Delicate, apple-green foliage and tiny,
clear white flowers heavy with stamens
on narrow/skinny stems.

perennial
height 1.5m (5ft)
1 per m² (10ft²)
flowers from early summer to late summer

4

Melica altissima 'Alba'
Siberian melic

A delicate, lime-green, deciduous grass
with gleaming, rice-like flowers.

grass
height 90cm (36in)
2 per m² (10ft²)
flowers from late spring to early summer

Good for...

bumblebees
solitary bees
hoverflies
butterflies
moths

In nature plants position themselves in response to subtle changes in the levels of moisture and light, the soil and topography of their location. This planting scheme reflects that, as *Pimpinella major* 'Rosea', *Astrantia* 'Roma', *Centranthus ruber* 'Albus' and *Aquilegia vulgaris* 'Munstead White' grow cheek by jowl and repeat, as if they have each chosen their own ideal spot. Umbels are the dominant flower shape in the wild, and here the chalky tones and delicate textures of the umbellifers *Pimpinella major* 'Rosea' and *Astrantia* 'Roma' are enlivened by *Sanguisorba menziesii* in jolting red. In the unexpected setting of a small space - this planting is next to a driveway - a looser planting inspired by nature has even greater impact. This scheme works well under a small tree such as a snowy mespilus (*Amelanchier × lamarckii*).

Method

1 Use a spade to dig over the soil to a crumbly consistency, breaking up any big lumps.

2 Gather together all the plants.

3 Start with the *Centranthus ruber* 'Albus', arranging the plants on the soil, still in their pots, and spacing them fairly far apart.

4 Add the *Astrantia* 'Roma', *Pimpinella major* 'Rosea' and *Sanguisorba menziesii* in ones and twos, letting the different plants nudge each other at their tips.

5 Finally, use the *Aquilegia vulgaris* 'White Munstead' to fill any occasional gaps.

6 When each plant has a spot, tap them out of their pots and loosen a few of the roots with your fingertips. Dig a hole for each plant to the same depth it was in its pot, then plant and gently firm the soil down using your hands. Water all the plants thoroughly.

Note: Aquilegias will self-sow readily, filling any spaces the following year.

The 5 plants

1

Aquilegia vulgaris 'Munstead White'

2

Astrantia 'Roma'

3

Centranthus ruber 'Albus'

4

Pimpinella major 'Rosea'

5

Sanguisorba menziesii

3

Centranthus ruber 'Albus'
**valerian
(white form)**

Pale but resilient
flowers on sturdy
stems. Sweet,
subtle scent.

perennial
height 80cm (32in)
1 per m² (10ft²)
*flowers from
early summer to
mid-autumn*

1

Aquilegia vulgaris 'Munstead White'
common columbine

Pale, angular, bell-shaped flowers.
A popular plant with garden designers.
An excitable self-seeder.

perennial
height 60cm (24in)
2 per m² (10ft²)
flowers from early summer to late summer

2

Astrantia 'Roma'
masterwort

Papery flowers in dusky pink with delicate
seedheads that last throughout winter.
Astra translates from the Latin as 'star',
reflecting the shape of the flowers.

perennial
height 60cm (24in)
3 per m² (10ft²)
flowers from late spring to early autumn

4

Pimpinella major 'Rosea'
pimpinella

Sugar-pink, airy
umbels. Popular
with small
pollinators that
have smaller
mouthparts.

perennial
height 90cm (36in)
3 per m² (10ft²)
*flowers from
early summer to
late summer*

5

Sanguisorba menziesii
Menzies' burnet

A fuzz of bright ruby-coloured burrs
on tall, wiry stems.

perennial
height 80cm (32in)
1 per m² (10ft²)
flowers from early summer to early autumn

Good for...

bumblebees
solitary bees
hoverflies
beetles
butterflies
ladybirds
lacewings and their hibernating larvae

This scheme is reminiscent of a woodland, but the plants have a fantastical feel. The open canopy and dappled shade of a single birch tree offer scope for a much wider choice of underplanting than a forest floor that is cool and dark.

The blue flowers of *Echinops ritro* 'Veitch's Blue', *Perovskia atriplicifolia* 'Blue Spire' and *Verbena bonariensis* are often described as 'bee-blue' since they are particularly attractive to bees which can see ultraviolet light. Bee-blue flowers such as these often have additional UV markings on their petals that act as signposts, guiding bees and other pollinators to the pollen and nectar inside. These are all tall plants, each with a small footprint, so they add easy height but take up little room, making them a good choice for a small garden.

Method

1 Gather together all the plants. If you can, choose the birch tree at a nursery rather than ordering it online and, before you buy, tip it out of its pot so you can examine the roots. Look for an even balance of root to compost, even if a few of the roots are starting to circle inside the pot.

2 In the garden, use a spade to dig over the soil to a crumbly consistency, breaking up any big lumps.

3 Position the birch tree where you would like it to grow and look at it from different angles, including though the windows of your home, to check the placement.

4 Dig a square hole a little deeper than the tree's pot and add a few spadefuls of peat-free, general-purpose compost.

5 Gently ease the tree out of its pot and loosen some of the roots with your fingertips. Plant the tree at the same depth it was in its pot and firm it in, using a booted foot.

6 Keeping the plants in their pots, space the *Echinops ritro* 'Veitch's Blue', *Lysimachia ephemerum* and *Perovskia atriplicifolia* 'Blue Spire' around the tree without getting too close to the trunk. Unless planting at the height of summer, they will be shorter than their full height, so imagine how they will look when they grow and aim for a balance of heights and forms, with some flowers jumping up near to others that are low.

7 Position the *Verbena bonariensis* next, threading the plants here and there to provide a ribbon of colour through the planting.

8 Tap each plant from its pot, winkling the roots out from the rootball a little with your fingertips. Dig the planting holes to the same depth each plant was in its pot, before planting and carefully firming into the soil with your hands.

9 Water all the plants thoroughly. Continue to water the roots of the birch tree regularly for up to six weeks while it settles in.

Note: Perovskia atriplicifolia 'Blue Spire' has white stems in winter that beautifully echo the white bark of the birch tree.

The 5 plants

1

Betula utilis var. *jacquemontii*

2

Echinops ritro 'Veitch's Blue'

3

Lysimachia ephemerum

4

Perovskia atriplicifolia 'Blue Spire'

5

Verbena bonariensis

3

*Lysimachia
ephemerum*
**willow-leaved
loosestrife**

Tall spires of small,
white flowers that
open from the
base to the tip on
consecutive days.

perennial
height 1m (39in)
2 per m² (10ft²)
*flowers from
early summer to
early autumn*

2

Echinops ritro 'Veitch's Blue'
globe thistle

Brilliant blue, spherical flowers that
evolve into striking, round seedheads.
Very popular with all types of bee.

perennial
height 1.2m (4ft)
1 per m² (10ft²)
flowers from mid-summer to late summer

1

Betula utilis var. *jacquemontii*
Himalayan birch

A small, deciduous tree with white
bark and an open, airy canopy.

tree
height 10m (33ft)
1 only
foliage only

4

Perovskia atriplicifolia 'Blue Spire'
Russian sage

Velvety, blue buds open to tiny, trumpet-like flowers on white stems. Warm and spicily scented.

perennial
height 1m (39in)
1 per m² (10ft²)
flowers from mid-summer to mid-autumn

5

Verbena bonariensis
verbena

Clusters of small, violet-blue flowers held at the tips of long, skinny stems. Useful for adding height in a small space. Easily grown from seed, if you wish.

perennial
height 2m (6½ft)
3 per m² (10ft²)
flowers from late spring to early autumn

Good for...

bumblebees
solitary bees
honeybees
hoverflies
butterflies
ladybirds
lacewings and their hibernating larvae

Flower gardens that are actively gardened have recently been found to be better for all kinds of wildlife than so-called 'wildlife gardens', with unkempt grass, a pond and wildflowers. This pretty design uses the forms and textures that we see in plants growing in the wild, with hints of an ancient hedgerow, but using cultivated plants. The umbellifers *Sambucus nigra* 'Black Beauty' and *Chaerophyllum hirsutum* 'Roseum' are perennials and so come back year after year, and here they are woven through with biennial foxgloves and sweet rocket. Although *Digitalis purpurea* 'Sutton's Delight' and *Hesperis matronalis* var. *albiflora* have a lifecycle of only two years, they gently self-sow, making themselves reliable in that way. *Polemonium caeruleum* is the bright blue flower.

The 5 plants

1
Chaerophyllum hirsutum 'Roseum'

2
Digitalis purpurea 'Sutton's Delight'

3
Hesperis matronalis var. *albiflora*

4
Polemonium caeruleum

5
Sambucus nigra 'Black Beauty'

Method

1 Use a spade to dig over the soil to a crumbly consistency, breaking up any big lumps.

2 Gather together all the plants.

3 Start with the umbellifers, the *Sambucus nigra* 'Black Beauty' and *Chaerophyllum hirsutum* 'Roseum'. These are among the tallest plants in the scheme, which works by creating layers of flowers at differing heights. Stand the plants on the soil in their pots, spacing them out randomly. Tall plants like these are useful at the back of the border, but can be even better at the front where other plants can be glimpsed through them.

4 In an ad hoc way, dot the *Hesperis matronalis* var. *albiflora* in between the *Sambucus* and *Chaerophyllum*. Leave plenty of room between each plant, so they have some space to grow into.

5 Thread through the *Digitalis purpurea* 'Sutton's Delight' as single plants between the *Sambucus*, *Chaerophyllum* and *Hesperis*. Keep stepping back to check the balance of the composition; the spaces between the foxglove spires of flowers are as important as the spires themselves. Rearrange and make any adjustments as you go.

6 Again, spacing the plants irregularly, add the blue *Polemonium caeruleum* in groups of two and three, and use some individual plants as outliers.

7 Tap each plant from its pot, easing the roots out a little with your fingertips. Dig a hole for each plant to the same depth it was in its pot before planting and gently firming down the soil with your hands. Water all the plants thoroughly.

Note: Hesperis matronalis var. *albiflora* is also straightforward to grow from seed, if you wish, which has the benefit of producing a good number of plants at little cost. Sow the seed in pots of compost in late summer to plant out the following spring.

1

Chaerophyllum hirsutum 'Roseum'
hairy chervil

Constellations of pale flowers atop deeply toothed green foliage. A cousin of wild cow parsley and also an indispensable plant for meadow-esque planting. In winter, the seedheads echo the shape of the former flowers.

perennial
height 50cm-1m (20-39in)
2 per m² (10ft²)
flowers from late spring to early summer

2

Digitalis purpurea 'Sutton's Delight'
foxglove

With tapering spires in muted colours, foxgloves take up little more room in the garden than the height of their flower spike. Brilliant for bees and other pollinators. Gently self-sows.

biennial
height 1.5m (5ft)
1 per m² (10ft²)
flowers from early summer to mid-summer

3

Hesperis matronalis var. *albiflora*
sweet rocket

Clear white flowers on a loose, airy plant. Sweet rocket flowers constantly for four months and even longer in a shaded spot. Easy to grow from seed and gently self-sows. Sweet scent.

biennial
height 90cm (36in)
3 per m² (10ft²)
flowers from late spring to early summer

5

Sambucus nigra 'Black Beauty'
purple-leaved elder

Umbrella umbels of tiny, pinkish-white
flowers on angular, blackcurrant-coloured
stems and dark purple foliage. Deciduous.

shrub
height 2.5m (8ft)
1 per m² (10ft²)
*flowers in early summer, but usually grown
for its dark foliage*

4

Polemonium caeruleum
Jacob's ladder

Small flowers in brightest blue atop tall
stems. The blue of the flowers is luminous
in a shaded spot. This is a popular plant
with garden designers.

perennial
height 90cm (36in)
3 per m² (10ft²)
flowers from early summer to mid-summer

Good for...

bumblebees
solitary bees
honeybees
hoverflies
butterflies
moths
tiny predator wasps (which eat aphids)
ladybirds
lacewings and their hibernating larvae

Garden designer Andy Sturgeon is known for his cool, industrial designs, including a garden inspired by the bony plates of a stegosaurus and another that takes its lead from the storage leaves of a bulb as it pushes into life. His own tiny garden in the middle of Brighton, in Sussex, England, fulfils the small/cool brief with considered design and beautiful planting and, unusually, it uses only one of each type of plant. Planted around a reflective water tank - the spout of water running into the tank also muffles the hum of nearby traffic - a medley of greens is woven with vibrant gems, including silver-metallic *Eryngium × zabelii* 'Big Blue', a giant-sized tulbaghia and the burnt orange spires of a designers' favourite: *Digitalis isabelliana* Bella ('Isob007'). You could also add a rota of different bulbs to flower throughout the year, if you wish.

The 5 plants

1

Digitalis isabelliana Bella ('Isob007')

2

Eryngium × zabelii 'Big Blue'

Method

1 Use a spade to dig over the soil to a crumbly consistency, breaking up any big lumps.

2 Have all the plants ready before you start planting.

3 Begin by positioning the *Salvia officinalis* and *Sesleria autumnalis*, still in their pots, which are used here for the contrasting patterns and textures provided by their foliage.

4 Add the *Digitalis isabelliana* Bella ('Isob007'), *Eryngium × zabelii* 'Big Blue' and *Tulbaghia* 'John May's Special', spacing them at irregular intervals. The spaces between the plants are just as important as the plants themselves.

5 Tap each plant from its pot and gently loosen a few of the roots with your fingertips. Dig a hole for each plant to the same depth it was in its pot before planting and gently firming in the soil with your hands.

6 Water all the plants thoroughly.

3

Salvia officinalis

4

Sesleria autumnalis

5

Tulbaghia 'John May's Special'

3

Salvia officinalis
sage

Grey/green, felty
leaves. Edible.
Warm and
spicily scented.

perennial
height 1m (39in)
1 per m² (10ft²)
*flowers from
late spring to
mid-summer*

2

Eryngium × *zabelii* 'Big Blue'
sea holly

Thimbles of blue thistle flowers and
sharply toothed, jagged foliage. Sea
holly turns more deeply blue in the heat
as summer progresses. Architectural
seedheads in winter echo the shapes of
the flowers.

perennial
height 70cm (28in)
1 per m² (10ft²)
flowers from early summer to late summer

1

Digitalis isabelliana Bella
('Isob007')
Canary Island foxglove

Tall spires of burnt orange flowers and
beautiful, architectural foliage.

perennial
height 1.2m (4ft)
1 per m² (10ft²)
flowers from early summer to mid-autumn

4

Sesleria autumnalis
autumn moor grass

A wiry clump of pale green leaves and tufts of silvery white flowers in summer. Evergreen.

grass
height 1.2m (4ft)
1 per m² (10ft²)
flowers from early summer to mid-autumn

5

Tulbaghia 'John May's Special'
society garlic

Big, pale umbels of symmetrical, trumpet-like flowers. Super-long-flowering perennial. A useful source of pollen and nectar for night-flying pollinators.

perennial
height 80cm (32in)
2 per m² (10ft²)
flowers from early summer to early autumn

Good for...

bumblebees
solitary bees
honeybees
hoverflies
butterflies
moths
ladybirds
lacewings and their hibernating larvae

Some plants are so easily grown from seed that it seems a shame not to give this a go. Most seed packets recommend sowing seed in spring, but you will get earlier flowering and bigger plants from an autumn sowing and spring planting. Achieving success is simply a case of giving the seeds what they need: light, warmth and water. Sow *Ammi majus*, *Digitalis purpurea* 'Pam's Choice' and *Hesperis matronalis* seeds in pots in autumn and keep them on a windowsill protected from winter's frosts, ready to plant out the following spring. You will also see the results of your efforts quickly, as the plants establish easily in the early spring soil. Poppies - in this case *Papaver commutatum* 'Ladybird' - add brightness and detail to a composition and are even easier to grow from seed. Scattered directly onto the soil, the seedlings will appear as soon as the weather starts to warm up.

Method

1 **In autumn** Gather together packets of *Ammi majus*, *Digitalis purpurea* 'Pam's Choice' and *Hesperis matronalis* seeds. Fill small pots with some seed compost, leaving a centimetre (half an inch) or so between the top of the compost and the rims of the pots for watering.

2 Tap each pot sharply on a flat surface to settle the compost and create a level surface. Sow the seed evenly, about 5-10 seeds to a pot. Allow enough space between seeds for the seedlings to germinate without crowding each other. Leave the seeds uncovered and water carefully using a gentle flow. Label each pot and place it on a windowsill. Keep the compost damp and look for shoots pushing up in two or three weeks.

3 When the seedlings have their first true leaves - the leaves of the plant itself rather than the 'seed leaves' which emerge first - move them into individual pots, taking care not to damage their delicate stems. Hold each seedling by a leaf and support the weight of the roots. Put the seedlings on a windowsill to grow on until you are ready to plant them.

4 **Outside** Use a spade to dig over the soil to a crumbly consistency, breaking up any big lumps. Dig holes and plant the *Allium christophii* bulbs, 15cm (6in) deep, with their pointy ends facing upwards. Cover the bulbs with soil and carefully tamp down.

5 **In spring** Starting with the *Hesperis matronalis* and *Ammi majus*, space the plants out on the soil, still in their pots, in pairs or in threes of each plant.

6 Add the *Digitalis purpurea* 'Pam's Choice' as individual specimens. These are tall plants and the space around them is as important as their flowers. Aim for an irregular rhythm among the rounded forms of the *Hesperis* and *Ammi*.

7 Tap each plant from its pot and ease out some of the roots using your fingertips. Dig a hole for each plant to the same depth it was in its pot, then plant and firm the soil down gently with your hands. Water all the plants thoroughly.

8 Take a scant pinch of *Papaver commutatum* 'Ladybird' seed and scatter this between the *Hesperis*, *Ammi* and *Digitalis*. Don't cover the seed, but water carefully and keep the soil damp if it doesn't rain. The seedlings will push up in two to four weeks.

The 5 plants

1

Allium christophii

2

Ammi majus

3

Digitalis purpurea 'Pam's Choice'

4

Hesperis matronalis

5

Papaver commutatum 'Ladybird'

1

Allium christophii
star of Persia

Violet, starburst flowers atop straight stems. In winter the seedheads repeat the shape of the flowers.

bulb
height 60cm (24in)
3 per m² (10ft²)
flowers from late spring to early summer

2

Ammi majus
bishop's flower

Like a round-flowered cow parsley, with tall, almost leafless stems and white umbels of flowers. Very popular with bees.

annual
height 1.2m (4ft)
2 per m² (10ft²)
flowers from early summer to early autumn

3

Digitalis purpurea 'Pam's Choice'
foxglove

Tapering spires of white flowers with blackcurrant speckles. Foxgloves take up little more room than their flower spikes and are useful for providing height. Very popular with bees and other flying pollinators.

biennial
height 1.2m (4ft)
1 per m² (10ft²)
flowers from late spring to mid-summer

4

Hesperis matronalis
sweet rocket

Sweetly scented, lilac flowers on a loose, airy plant. An easy plant to grow from seed and will gently self-sow.

biennial
height 90cm (36in)
3 per m² (10ft²)
flowers from late spring to early summer

5

Papaver commutatum 'Ladybird'
poppy

Brilliant red flowers with a black spot on each petal. Will self-seed freely, providing a seedbank to flower in subsequent years.

annual
height 45cm (18in)
10 per m² (10ft²)
flowers from early summer to late summer

Good for...

bumblebees
solitary bees
hoverflies
caterpillars
butterflies
moths

Alliums are one of the most reliably perennial bulbs, which makes them ideal candidates for layered planting. Here, the quirkily tall *Allium* 'Summer Drummer' provides the upper layer to an understorey of *Orlaya grandiflora, Fagopyrum dibotrys* and colour-pop poppies that push through at mid-height. The eccentricity of the alliums' towering stems and their metallic buds gives the composition a contemporary feel. The poppy, an annual with fairly fleeting flowers, will self-seed excitedly, filling the gaps and coming back each year. I like this combination against the rusty, corrugated iron backdrop, but it would work equally well against a darkly stained fence.

Method

1 **In autumn** Use a spade to dig over the soil to a crumbly consistency, breaking up any big lumps. These plants all enjoy sharp drainage, so dig in a few spadefuls of horticultural grit, too.

2 Plant the *Allium* 'Summer Drummer' bulbs, burying them 10-15cm (4-6in) deep and with their pointy ends facing upwards.

3 **In spring** Start with the *Iris* 'Italic Light'. These are the chunkiest plants in the scheme and need more careful placement than the open, transparent plants. Think about how plants arrange themselves in nature, responding to subtle changes in light and shade. Stand the irises on the soil, still in their pots, spacing them out in an irregular pattern.

4 Tap each iris from its pot and ease out the roots a little with your fingertips. Dig a hole for each one. Take care not to plant each iris too deeply, as the top of the rhizome (the woody stem that looks like a root) should be kept above the soil. Firm the plants in gently using your hands.

5 Add the *Orlaya grandiflora* and *Fagopyrum dibotrys* in twos and threes of each type, allowing the different species to overlap at their boundaries. Step back to check the balance of the composition, looking for layers of different heights and making adjustments as you go. As for the iris, tap each plant from its pot and ease out some of the roots with your fingertips. Dig a hole for each plant to the same depth it was in its pot, plant and firm in gently with your hands. Water all the plants thoroughly.

6 Poppies are best grown from seed sown straight onto the soil, as they dislike being transplanted. Use a stick to mark a circle on the ground where you want them to grow and scatter a scant pinch of seed, following the line you have marked. This will help you identify the seedlings when they push up.

7 Cover the seeds with soil and water carefully. If it doesn't rain, keep the soil damp and look out for green shoots pushing up in one or two weeks.

Note: Alliums have architectural seedheads in winter that echo the shape of the flowers.

The 5 plants

1

Allium 'Summer Drummer'

2

Fagopyrum dibotrys

3

Iris 'Italic Light'

4

Orlaya grandiflora

5

Papaver rhoeas

3

Iris 'Italic Light'
bearded iris

A straightforward
iris in middling
purple that isn't
too fussy.

perennial
height 90cm (36in)
2 per m² (10ft²)
*flowers from late
spring to early
summer*

2

Fagopyrum dibotrys
tall buckwheat

A tall plant with panicles of gauzy,
white flowers.

perennial
height 1.5m (5ft)
2 per m² (10ft²)
flowers from late summer to early autumn

1

Allium 'Summer Drummer'
ornamental onion

A very tall allium. The metallic buds
open to chalky pink, starburst flowers.
Architectural seedheads in winter.

bulb
height 2m (6½ft)
5 per m² (10ft²)
flowers from mid-summer to early autumn

4

Orlaya
grandiflora
white laceflower

Pure white flowers
in airy umbels on
near-leafless stems.

annual
height 60cm (24in)
3 per m² (10ft²)
flowers from
early summer to
early autumn

5

Papaver rhoeas
common poppy

Clear red flowers with jet-black middles.
Easily grown from seed and an excitable
self-seeder.

annual
height 75cm (30in)
5 per m² (10ft²)
flowers from early summer to mid-summer

Good for...

bumblebees
solitary bees
hoverflies
butterflies

English flower garden

June | Early summer

This plan riffs on the concept of an English flower garden but in a small space, using a layered mixture of perennial and annual plants. *Cirsium heterophyllum* and *Phlomis tuberosa* 'Amazone' are threaded with foxgloves, corncockles and the dainty, white flowers of the umbellifer *Orlaya grandiflora*. The rocketing flowers of the foxgloves offer height but take up little room in the soil, while *Orlaya grandiflora*'s airy frame and almost leafless stems make it particularly useful for tucking in between the other plants.

Add some foxglove plants, the *Digitalis purpurea*, towards the front and back of the border, rather than just in the middle, and include a few as outliers. This replicates how they arrange themselves in nature on the edge of a woodland where they can take best advantage of available light.

Method

1 Use a spade to dig over the soil to a crumbly consistency, breaking up any big lumps.

2 Gather together the *Phlomis tuberosa* 'Amazone', *Cirsium heterophyllum*, *Orlaya grandiflora*, *Digitalis purpurea* and a packet of *Agrostemma githago* 'Alba' seeds.

3 Starting with the *Phlomis* and *Cirsium*, space the plants out on the soil, still in their pots.

4 Thread the *Orlaya* and most of the *Digitalis* between the *Phlomis* and *Cirsium*, keeping in mind that they will grow into quite chunky plants.

5 Dot the remaining *Digitalis* here and there as single plants, with some at the front and some at the back of the border.

6 Tap each plant out of its pot and loosen a few of the roots with your fingertips. Dig a hole for each plant to the same depth it was in its pot before planting and carefully firming down the soil with your hands. Water all the plants thoroughly.

7 *Agrostemma githago* 'Alba' are best grown from seed sown straight onto the soil, as they dislike being transplanted. Use a stick to mark a circle on the ground where you want them to grow and sow a scant pinch of seed, following the line you have marked. This will help you identify the seedlings when they eventually push up.

8 Cover the *Agrostemma* seeds with soil and water gently, making an effort not to dislodge them. If it doesn't rain, keep the soil damp and look out for their green shoots pushing up in one or two weeks.

The 5 plants

1

Agrostemma githago 'Alba'

2

Cirsium heterophyllum

3

Digitalis purpurea

4

Orlaya grandiflora

5

Phlomis tuberosa 'Amazone'

3

Digitalis purpurea
foxglove

Tapering spires of muted pink flowers that are darker on the inside and speckled. Each floret is big enough for a large bumblebee to crawl completely inside. Gently self-sows.

short-lived perennial
height 2m (6½ft)
1 per m² (10ft²)
flowers from early summer to mid-summer

1

Agrostemma githago 'Alba'
corncockle

Delicate, round, white flowers atop near-leafless stems.

annual
height 1.2m (4ft)
1 per m² (10ft²)
flowers from early summer to mid-autumn

2

Cirsium heterophyllum
melancholy thistle

A pink form of the wild thistle, with jagged leaves and dusky pink flowers. Very popular with bees.

perennial
height 1.2m (4ft)
2 per m² (10ft²)
flowers from early summer to late summer

4

Orlaya
grandiflora
white laceflower

Pure white flowers
held in big, airy
umbels on almost
leafless stems.

annual
height 60cm (24in)
3 per m² (10ft²)
flowers from
early summer to
early autumn

5

Phlomis tuberosa 'Amazone'
sage-leaf mullein

Felted leaves and whorls of pink flowers
on vertical stems. In winter the seedheads
echo the shape of the flowers.

perennial
height 1.2m (4ft)
1 per m² (10ft²)
flowers from mid-summer to late summer

Good for...

bumblebees
solitary bees
honeybees
hoverflies
butterflies
ladybirds
hibernating lacewing larvae

Succulent bowl

June

Early summer

Succulents are the 'marmite' of plants, which is perhaps due to the many sorry-looking specimens seen in jam jars on café tables. In contrast, this pot celebrates the vibrancy and detail of their flowers in a collection reminiscent of the bowls of floating hellebores you see in smart hotels. All succulents will flower in the beating sun, often with richly coloured, highly stylized flowers. My favourite, *Echeveria elegans*, has pink, elongated stalks and lovely flamingo-pink flowers. *Aloe aristata*'s orange flowers hover like an exotic bird over reptilian foliage, and the pebble-like leaves of *Sempervivum calcareum* are topped with white flowers.

Method

1 Gather together the plants. Succulents need very little space for their roots, but sharp drainage is vital, so choose a shallow dish or bowl and drill some holes in the base if there aren't some already. This concrete bowl works beautifully against the chunky leaves of the succulents. It's also portable, making it easy to place the succulents in the sunniest spot. When the flowers fade, the plants become a study in form and texture.

2 Combine two handfuls of horticultural grit with a handful of peat-free, general-purpose compost to make a beautifully open mix. Place a pebble over the drainage hole(s) of the bowl to keep the gritty compost inside.

3 Mound up the gritty compost in the bowl to create a hump that is a few centimetres (an inch or so) higher in the middle than at the rim.

4 Arrange the plants, thinking about how their textures match and mismatch. Remove the plants from their pots and nestle each one in. The roots will find their own way down.

5 Fill any gaps between the plants by snapping off small rosettes and tucking them in where needed. Remove them from the parent plants by twisting them between your thumb and forefinger.

6 Use a little more grit to cover any remaining compost. This will also keep the roots cool and dark. Water once, sparingly. Subsequently, drench the bowl only once or twice a year in the height of summer.

Note: These plants need very few nutrients and can create what they need from their own withering lower leaves.

The 5 plants

1

Aloe aristata

2

Echeveria elegans

3

Sedum 'Silver Roses'

4

Sempervivum calcareum

5

Sempervivum 'Gulle Dame'

1

Aloe aristata
torch plant

Reptilian-looking
leaves prickled
with white and
luminous, citrus-
yellow flowers.

perennial
height 25cm (10in)
1 per pot
*flowers from
late summer to
early autumn*

2

Echeveria elegans
Mexican gem

Squidgy, pebble-like leaves topped
with brilliant pink stalks and flowers.

perennial
height 15cm (6in)
1 per pot
flowers from early summer to late summer

3

Sedum
'Silver Roses'
stonecrop

Pale green, pebble-
like leaves unfurl
like a rosebud.
Milky white flowers
in summer.

perennial
height 5cm (2in)
1 per pot
*flowers from
early summer to
late summer*

4

Sempervivum calcareum
houseleek

Sharply pointed, flattish leaves tipped with red.

perennial
height 15cm (6in)
1 per pot
flowers from early summer to mid-summer

5

Sempervivum 'Gulle Dame'
houseleek

Vibrant whorls of carmine leaves.

perennial
height 90cm (36in)
1 per pot
flowers from late spring to early summer

Good for...

bumblebees
solitary bees
hoverflies
butterflies

This planting scheme for the shadowy area at the foot of a wall uses five plants that come botanically close to wild plants. Plants like these exude a light and airy feel as they have a higher ratio of stem and leaf to petal and flower. The tall, hovering umbels of *Cenolophium denudatum* echo the shapes of the lower-growing *Astrantia major* 'Large White' flowers and also the height of the foxglove, *Digitalis lutea*. *Alchemilla mollis*, a low, green filler plant, holds a single, light-reflecting raindrop in each serrated leaf after a shower of rain. Even though it's in the shadows, this composition feels uplifting and light.

Method

1 Use a spade to dig over the soil to a crumbly consistency, breaking up any big lumps. These plants will also appreciate the addition of a few spadefuls of peat-free, general-purpose compost to replicate the humus-rich conditions they favour.

2 Have all the plants ready before you start.

3 The plants work as a whole and the planting is a case of putting them together in such a way that it feels as if they have spontaneously colonized the planting area - in this case, the base of a wall. Begin with the textural plants, the lower-growing *Astrantia major* and *Alchemilla mollis*, arranging them cheek by jowl, still in their pots, as if they have colonized the foot of the wall.

4 Next, add the *Cenolophium denudatum* and *Thalictrum delavayi* 'Album' as an upper layer and then the *Digitalis lutea* towards the back of the composition.

5 Tap each plant from its pot and tease out the roots a little with your fingertips. Dig a hole for each plant to the same depth it was in its pot, then plant and gently firm down the soil with your hands.

6 Water all the plants thoroughly.

The 5 plants

1

Alchemilla mollis

2

Astrantia major 'Large White'

3

Cenolophium denudatum

4

Digitalis lutea

5

Thalictrum delavayi 'Album'

1

Alchemilla mollis
lady's mantle

Textural, serrated foliage and a haze of bright, citrus-lemon flowers.

perennial
height 60cm (24in)
1 per m² (10ft²)
flowers from early summer to early autumn

2

Astrantia major 'Large White'
Hattie's pincushion

White, papery umbels that evolve into architectural seedheads in winter. *Astra* translates from the Latin as 'star', reflecting the shape of the flowers.

perennial
height 60cm (24in)
3 per m² (10ft²)
flowers from late spring to early autumn

3

Cenolophium denudatum
Baltic parsley

Big umbels of tiny, white flowers on tall, angular stems.

perennial
height 1m (39in)
1 per m² (10ft²)
flowers from mid-summer to mid-autumn

4

Digitalis lutea
**small yellow
foxglove**

Delicate spires of
small, loosely held,
primrose-yellow
flowers. Unlike
most foxgloves,
this is reliably
perennial. Popular
with bees.

perennial
height 60cm (24in)
1 per m² (10ft²)
*flowers from
late spring to
mid-summer*

5

Thalictrum delavayi 'Album'
meadow rue

Airy foliage in apple-green and small,
pale flowers.

perennial
height 1.5m (5ft)
1 per m² (10ft²)
flowers from early summer to late summer

Good for...

bumblebees
solitary bees
honeybees
hoverflies
butterflies
damsel bugs
shield bugs
ladybirds
hibernating lacewing larvae

Fieldwork

An annual meadow might not feel like the obvious choice for a small garden, but even one square metre (ten square feet) of soil is enough to capture a sense of the wild in a city plot. The urban/bucolic juxtaposition is best epitomized in the work of garden designer Nigel Dunnett in the colourful meadow-esque planting he designed for the brutalist architecture of the Barbican Estate and the Queen Elizabeth Olympic Park, both in London.

Colour-pop poppies are fairly fleeting flowers, but they self-sow in good numbers, making themselves reliable. All of these plants are hugely popular with pollinators.

Method

1 You can sow wildflower seeds in spring or in autumn, into the last lingering warmth of the soil. You will get earlier flowering and bigger plants from an autumn sowing.

2 Use a spade to dig over the soil to a crumbly consistency, breaking up any big lumps.

3 Tip the seeds from each packet into a bowl and mix them together.

4 Scatter a scant pinch of the mixed seed over each square metre (10 square feet) of soil.

5 Scuff the surface a bit using your hands to ensure that the seeds make good contact with the soil.

6 Water the seeds gently and keep the soil damp if it doesn't rain until green shoots push up in one or two weeks.

Note: All these plants have the advantage of self-sowing and flowering again in varying numbers in subsequent years.

The 5 plants

1

Ammi majus

2

Centaurea cyanus

3

Cosmos bipinnatus 'Purity'

4

Echium vulgare

5

Papaver rhoeas

1

Ammi majus
bishop's flower

Similar to cow parsley with tall, almost leafless stems and open umbel flowers. Very popular with bees and small pollinators.

annual
height 1.2m (4ft)
1 packet of seed
flowers from early summer to early autumn

2

Centaurea cyanus
cornflower

Brilliant blue flowers with pinked edges.

annual
height 90cm (36in)
1 packet of seed
flowers from mid-summer to mid-autumn

3

Cosmos bipinnatus 'Purity'
cosmos

Daisy-like flowers and good grown in close company due to the delicate foliage. Easy to grow from seed.

annual
height 1.8m (6ft)
1 packet of seed
flowers from mid-summer to late summer

4

Echium vulgare
viper's bugloss

Bristly foliage and spikes of small, bright blue flowers.

annual
height 80cm (32in)
1 packet of seed
flowers from early summer to mid-autumn

5

Papaver rhoeas
common poppy

Bright red flowers with black centres.

annual
height 75cm (30in)
1 packet of seed
flowers from early summer to mid-summer

Good for...

bumblebees
solitary bees
honeybees
hoverflies
butterflies
day- and night-flying moths
damsel bugs
shield bugs
ladybirds
lacewings

Salvias are sometimes described as 'bee-blue' because they are easily spotted by insects on the wing. The ultraviolet markings on their petals that are invisible to us act as street markings to bees - chevrons and arrows guiding them to the nectar inside. When a bee crawls inside a *Salvia nemorosa* 'Caradonna' floret, for example, the weight of the bee activates a trigger that makes the stamens curl down and deposit a blob of pollen on the bee's back which is exactly positioned to pollinate the next flower it visits. In this plan for a sunny space, it is matched with other plants that are popular with pollinators, including a tall, flat-headed *Achillea* 'Coronation Gold' and the petal-packed, pincushion-like flowers of *Knautia macedonica*. *Galtonia candicans*, a perennial bulb with luminous white flowers that threads between the other plants, is an ideal candidate for the layered planting.

The 5 plants

Method

1 Use a spade to dig over the soil to a crumbly consistency, breaking up any big lumps.

2 Gather together the plants.

3 Starting with the *Salvia nemorosa* 'Caradonna', stand the plants on the soil, still in their pots, to make a block of colour.

4 Add the *Achillea* 'Coronation Gold' and *Knautia macedonica* to the arrangement, using the same broad brushstrokes. These are good mutual company as they grow in a similar same way and at a similar pace.

5 Next, add the *Euphorbia wallichii*.

6 Adjust one or two of the plants at the edges of each group, so they will thread together a little as they grow.

7 Tap each plant from its pot and tease out the roots a little with your fingertips. Dig a hole for each plant to the same depth it was in its pot, then plant and gently firm the soil down with your hands.

8 Water all the plants thoroughly.

Note: Galtonia candicans is best planted as dormant bulbs. Plant the bulbs with their pointy ends facing upwards just below the surface of the soil in late winter.

1

Achillea 'Coronation Gold'

2

Euphorbia wallichii

3

Galtonia candicans

4

Knautia macedonica

5

Salvia nemorosa 'Caradonna'

1

Achillea 'Coronation Gold'
yarrow

Tall, yellow, flat-headed flowers and feathery foliage. The striking seedheads are architectural in winter and echo the shape of the flowers.

perennial
height 80cm (32in)
3 per m² (10ft²)
flowers from early summer to late summer

2

Euphorbia wallichii
spurge

Bright green leaves and clear yellow flowers. Airy and useful for structure.

perennial
height 60cm (24in)
2 per m² (10ft²)
flowers from late spring to late summer

3

Galtonia candicans
summer hyacinth

A bulb with luminous, waxy, white flowers. Subtle scent.

bulb
height 1.2m (4ft)
2 per m² (10ft²)
flowers from early summer to early autumn

5

Salvia nemorosa 'Caradonna'
Balkan clary

Upright spikes of inky flowers dotted
on near-black stems. Jam-packed with
pollen and nectar for pollinators.

perennial
height 60cm (24in)
3 per m² (10ft²)
flowers from early summer to mid-autumn

4

Knautia macedonica
Macedonian scabious

A colourful, cultivated member of the
thistle family with jagged leaves and a
good number of flowers. This is one of
the longest flowering perennial plants
and with the highest flower count.

perennial
height 1.5m (5ft)
2 per m² (10ft²)
flowers from mid-summer to early autumn

Good for...

bumblebees
solitary bees
honeybees
hoverflies
butterflies
moths
hibernating ladybirds and
lacewing larvae

Colour is a potent tool in the garden and this plan plays with a pretty, muted palette that encapsulates the freshness of summer. Deliciously cool *Campanula lactiflora* is set off beautifully by the copper flowers of *Digitalis parviflora*, a flower form that hints at the woodland. *Salvia nemorosa* 'Caradonna' adds visual heft. Citrus-yellow *Euphorbia seguieriana* lifts the whole scheme, its flowers a bright note even on grey days.

The 5 plants

1
Briza media

2
Campanula lactiflora

3
Digitalis parviflora

4
Euphorbia seguieriana

5
Salvia nemorosa 'Caradonna'

Method

1 Use a spade to dig over the soil to a crumbly consistency, breaking up any big lumps.

2 Gather together all the plants.

3 Start with the darkest plant, the *Salvia nemorosa* 'Caradonna', standing them, still in their pots, on the soil in small groups.

4 Next to the *Salvia*, add the *Euphorbia seguieriana* and then the *Digitalis parviflora*.

5 Position *the Campanula lactiflora* next to the occasional *Digitalis*.

6 Thread the *Briza media* grasses between the flowering plants, using the ribbon-like leaves to 'stitch' the composition together.

7 Tap each plant from its pot and ease out the roots a little with your fingertips. Dig a hole for each plant to the same depth it was in its pot, then plant and firm down the soil gently with your hands.

8 Water all the plants thoroughly.

3

Digitalis
parviflora
small-flowered
foxglove

Jam-packed with
copper flowers that
open from base to
tip. A tall plant with
a small footprint
in the soil. Very
popular with bees.

perennial
height 60cm (24in)
1 per m² (10ft²)
flowers from late
spring to mid-
summer

1

Briza media
lesser quaking grass

Bright green leaves and fat flower buds
suspended in the air like a swarm of bees.
Tiny, white flowers. Semi-evergreen.

grass
height 50cm (20in)
1 per m² (10ft²)
flowers from late spring to mid-summer

2

Campanula lactiflora
milky bellflower

Loose panicles of sky-blue flowers held on
a tall, airy plant.

perennial
height 1m (39in)
1 per m² (10ft²)
flowers from mid-summer to early autumn

4

Euphorbia seguieriana
Sequier's spurge

Bright citrus-lime foliage and citrus-yellow flowers.

perennial
height 80cm (32in)
1 per m² (10ft²)
flowers from early summer to late summer

5

Salvia nemorosa 'Caradonna'
Balkan clary

Upright spikes of dark inky-blue flowers on almost-black stems. Packed with pollen and nectar.

perennial
height 60cm (24in)
3 per m² (10ft²)
flowers from early summer to mid-autumn

Good for...

bumblebees
solitary bees
honeybees
hoverflies
butterflies
moths

Mathiasella bupleuroides 'Green Dream' has an intriguing flower: a big, green umbel. In this large zinc pot I have matched its architectural foliage with two grasses - *Melica altissima* 'Alba' and *Hakonechloa macra* - with *Erigeron karvinskianus* and *Amsonia tabernaemontana*, which has pale blue flowers in late summer.

The two grasses grow to the same height, but flower consecutively from late spring to early autumn. *Hakonechloa macra* is particularly slow growing and so useful in a pot, and I like the way the tiny flowers of *Melica altissima* 'Alba' are echoed by the raindrops held on its leaves after a shower of rain. The height and detailing of the zinc pot further emphasizes the linear nature of the planting.

Method

1 Gather together all the plants. Choose a big pot and put it in position before you start work, as once filled with compost it will be heavy and difficult to move.

2 Drill some drainage holes in the base of the pot if there aren't some already. Cover the holes with a pebble to keep the compost inside.

3 Fill the pot with a good-quality, peat-free, general-purpose compost, leaving about a centimetre (half an inch) or so between the top of the compost and the rim for watering.

4 Plant the two *Mathiasella bupleuroides* 'Green Dream' first, positioning them towards the middle of the pot. Tap each plant from its pot, ease out a few of the roots with your fingertips and plant to the same depth it was in its pot. Gently firm in using your hands.

5 Add the grasses next, the *Hakonechloa macra* and *Melica altissima* 'Alba', spacing them evenly to thread together as they grow.

6 Next add the *Amsonia tabernaemontana* and carefully firm them in. Dot the *Erigeron karvinskianus* at irregular intervals around the edges of the pot.

7 Use your fingers to tuck some extra compost in between each of the plants to fill any spaces in the pot. Water thoroughly.

Note: Plants grown in pots need considerably more water than those in the soil. Water once a week and every day during the heat of summer.

The 5 plants

1

Amsonia tabernaemontana

2

Erigeron karvinskianus

3

Hakonechloa macra

4

Mathiasella bupleuroides 'Green Dream'

5

Melica altissima 'Alba'

1

Amsonia tabernaemontana
eastern bluestar

Tall stems with loose panicles of dainty,
sky-blue flowers.

perennial
height 80cm (32in)
2 per pot
flowers from early summer to late summer

2

Erigeron karvinskianus
Mexican fleabane

Tumbling, daisy-like flowers with yellow
centres. Gently self-sows.

perennial
height 30cm (12in)
2 per pot
flowers from mid-spring to late autumn

3

*Hakonechloa
macra*
**Japanese
forest grass**

Green, deciduous
grass with small,
lime-green flowers.
Grows slowly,
making a clump.

grass
height 30cm (12in)
2 per pot
*flowers from late
summer to early
autumn, but usually
grown for its foliage*

4

*Mathiasella
bupleuroides*
'Green Dream'
mathiasella

Bright apple-
green umbels
and architectural
foliage. The florets
are large enough
for a bumblebee
to crawl inside.
Striking seedheads
follow the flowers
in winter.

bulb
height 1m (39in)
2 per pot
*flowers from
mid-spring to
early summer*

5

Melica altissima 'Alba'
Siberian melic

Bright green, deciduous grass with shiny,
rice-like flowers and tiny, pale seedheads.

grass
height 90cm (36in)
2 per pot
flowers from late spring to early summer

Good for...

bumblebees
solitary bees
honeybees
hoverflies
butterflies
moths
shield bugs
ladybirds
hibernating lacewing larvae

Many of us recognize that we are only ever the custodian of our garden and that for the time we are in charge we have a responsibility to do our best for it, using local materials wherever possible and choosing plants that are a good fit for the soil we have. This planting scheme, by garden designer Jo McKerr, unpicks the details of an existing space - hot, sunny and rubble-filled following building work - to make a garden that is beautiful, colourful and sustainable in equal measure. It is less about the individual plants and more about how they work together, and the plants flower all summer long with little recourse to the watering can. The informality of this combination belies its resilient nature. In winter, *Eryngium × zabelii* 'Jos Eijking' and *Phlomis russeliana* evolve into architectural seedheads that echo the shape of the flowers.

The 5 plants

Method

1 Use a spade to dig over the soil to a crumbly consistency, breaking up any big lumps.

2 Gather together all the plants.

3 This angular, pared-back approach relies on the rhythm of the plants as much as the plants themselves. Space the *Phlomis russeliana* and *Eryngium × zabelii* 'Jos Eijking' out on the soil, still in their pots, arranging them singly and, occasionally, in like-with-like pairs.

4 Thread the *Verbena officinalis* var. *grandiflora* 'Bampton' in between the *Phlomis* and *Eryngium* in an irregular pattern.

5 Dot the *Oenothera biennis* here and there individually to provide points of colour.

6 When you are happy with the arrangement, tap the plants from their pots and tease out some of the roots slightly using your fingertips. Dig a hole for each plant to the same depth it was in its pot, then plant and firm down the soil gently with your hands.

7 Water all the plants thoroughly.

8 It is best to grow *Allium sphaerocephalon* in autumn from dormant bulbs to flower the following year. Bury the bulbs 10-15cm (4-6in) deep and with their pointy ends facing upwards, tucking them between the other plants. You can also buy them as budding bulbs in early summer, if you prefer.

Note: In winter *Eryngium × zabellii* 'Jos Eijking' and *Phlomis russeliana* evolve into architectural seedheads that echo the shape of the original flowers.

1

Allium sphaerocephalon

2

Eryngium × zabelii 'Jos Eijking'

3

Oenothera biennis

4

Phlomis russeliana

5

Verbena officinalis var. *grandiflora* 'Bampton'

1

Allium sphaerocephalon
round-headed allium

Round, blackcurrant-coloured flowers atop
straight, green stems and skinny foliage.

bulb
height 90cm (36in)
8 per m² (10ft²)
flowers from mid-summer to late summer

2

Eryngium × zabelii 'Jos Eijking'
sea holly

Electric-blue thistle flowers inside sharp
bracts and jagged leaves with sharp 'teeth'.
The flowers turn progressively more blue
as summer progresses.

perennial
height 70cm (28in)
1 per m² (10ft²)
flowers from late summer to mid-autumn

3

*Oenothera
biennis*
evening primrose

Butter-yellow
flowers that open at
dusk. Subtle scent.

biennial
height 1.5m (5ft)
1 per m² (10ft²)
*flowers from
mid-summer
to late summer*

4

Phlomis russeliana
phlomis

Whorls of bright yellow flowers on poker-straight stems. In winter, the seedheads echo the shape of the flowers.

perennial
height 1.2m (4ft)
1 per m² (10ft²)
flowers from mid-summer to late summer

5

Verbena officinalis var. *grandiflora* 'Bampton'
vervain

Tiny, pink, trumpet-like flowers at the tips of arching stems. The leaves are serrated and tinged with plum.

perennial
height 1m (39in)
1 per m² (10ft²)
flowers from early summer to mid-autumn

Good for...

bumblebees
solitary bees
hoverflies
butterflies
moths
ladybirds
hibernating lacewing larvae

Poppies are fairly fleeting flowers, yet they are easily grown from seed and self-sow readily, making themselves reliable in that respect. This plan is inspired by the Californium Superbloom - a mass wild flowering phenomenon in California's Death Valley where unusually high numbers of dormant wildflower seeds germinate and flower at the same time - which has become a mecca for horticulturalists and social media influencers alike.

The Californian poppy, *Eschscholzia californica*, favours sun and scratchier soil, making it a good choice for the UK's shifting weather patterns. It flowers from early summer.

Method

1 You can sow wildflower seeds in spring or in autumn, into the last lingering warmth of the soil. You will get slightly earlier flowering and bigger plants from an autumn sowing.

2 Use a spade to dig over the soil to a crumbly consistency, breaking up any big lumps.

3 Mix the seeds together in a pot and cast a scant pinch onto the surface of the soil. Scuff the soil a bit, but don't cover the seeds.

4 Water the seeds gently. If it doesn't rain, keep the soil damp until green shoots start to push up in about a week's time.

Note: All these plants will self-sow, flowering in subsequent years.

The 5 plants

1

Eschscholzia californica

2

Eschscholzia californica 'Carmine King'

3

Glebionis segetum

4

Linaria 'Peachy'

5

Linum grandiflorum var. *rubrum*

3

Glebionis segetum
corn marigold

A once familiar sight in a British cornfield. Yellow, daisy-like flowers on tall stems. Easily grown from seed.

annual
height 80cm (32in)
1 packet of seed
flowers from early summer to early autumn

2

Eschscholzia californica
'Carmine King'
Californian poppy

Rosy-pink buds unfold into pale flowers. Pinching off faded flowers encourages more. Easily grown from seed.

annual
height 45cm (18in)
1 packet of seed
flowers from early summer to early autumn

1

Eschscholzia californica
Californian poppy

Tangerine flowers followed by long, curved seedheads. Pinching off the faded flowers encourages further blooms. Easily grown from seed.

annual
height 45cm (18in)
1 packet of seed
flowers from early summer to early autumn

4

Linaria 'Peachy'
toadflax

Pale snapdragon-like flowers on gently curving stems. Easily grown from seed.

perennial
height 90cm (36in)
1 packet of seed
flowers from early summer to mid-autumn

5

Linum grandiflorum var. *rubrum*
scarlet flax

Scarlet flowers with deeper-coloured middles. Easily grown from seed.

annual
height 50cm (20in)
1 packet of seed
flowers from early summer to early autumn

Good for...

bumblebees
solitary bees
honeybees
hoverflies
butterflies
day- and night-flying moths

A space planted as a cutting patch is the most sustainable way to grow fresh flowers for the home, without the environmental impact of airmiles and single-use cellophane wraps. Dahlias grow in a painter's palette of colours and they thrive on being cut regularly and often. Annuals, such as *Ammi majus* and *Orlaya grandiflora*, produce as many flowers and seeds as possible in the shortest space of time. Cut *Ammi*, *Orlaya* and *Dahlia* flowers just above their leaf joints to encourage new buds to form. Always cut flowers either early in the morning or late in the evening for longer-lasting blooms and cut them straight into a bucket of water.

Method

1 **In autumn** Gather together packets of *Ammi majus* and *Orlaya grandiflora* seeds. Fill small pots with some seed compost, leaving a centimetre (half an inch) or so between the top of the compost and the rims of the pots for watering.

2 Tap each pot sharply on a flat surface to settle the compost and create a level surface for sowing. Sow the seed evenly, 5-10 seeds to a pot, and leave enough space between them for the seedlings to grow without crowding each other. Leave the seeds uncovered and water using a gentle flow rather than a gush of water. Label each pot and place it on a windowsill. Keep the compost damp and shoots will push up in two to three weeks.

3 When the seedlings have their first true leaves - the leaves of the plant itself rather than the initial 'seed leaves' - transfer them to individual pots. Take care not to damage the delicate stems - hold each seedling by a leaf and support the weight of the roots. Keep on a windowsill.

4 **Outside** Use a spade to dig the soil over to a crumbly consistency, breaking up any big lumps. Dig holes, 15cm (6in) deep, and bury each *Allium stipitatum* ' Mount Everest' bulb with its pointy end facing upwards. Cover the bulbs with soil and tamp down.

5 **In spring** Tap the dahlias from their pots and loosen a few of the roots with your fingertips. Dig a hole for each plant to the same depth it was in its pot. Dahlias are hungry plants, so add a spadeful of peat-free, general-purpose compost to their holes before planting and firming down the soil gently with your hands. Thread the *Ammi* and *Orlaya* seedlings around the dahlias. Water thoroughly.

The 5 plants

1

Allium stipitatum 'Mount Everest'

2

Ammi majus

3

Dahlia 'Blue Bayou'

4

Dahlia 'Frank Holmes'

5

Orlaya grandiflora

1

Allium stipitatum 'Mount Everest'
ornamental onion

White starburst flowers sit atop straight, green stems. The spherical seedheads are striking and repeat the shape of the flowers.

bulb
height 1.2m (4ft)
1 per m² (10ft²)
flowers from early summer to mid-summer

2

Ammi majus
bishop's flower

Like an airy cow parsley with tall, almost leafless stems and umbel flowers. Very popular with bees.

annual
height 1.2m (4ft)
1 per m² (10ft²)
flowers from early summer to early autumn

3

Dahlia 'Blue Bayou'
dahlia

Anemone-flowered dahlia with an intensely pink, open flower. Long stems and long-lasting flowers in the garden and when cut. Unusually for a dahlia, this is good for pollinators.

perennial
height 1.2m (4ft)
1 per per m² (10ft²)
flowers from mid-summer to early autumn

4

Dahlia 'Frank Holmes'
dahlia

Architectural, pompom flowers in good numbers.

perennial
height 90cm (36in)
1 per m² (10ft²)
flowers from mid-summer to early autumn

Note: At the start of winter heap another spadeful of compost on top of the soil above dahlia tubers to protect them from the coldest weather, so they will flower again the following year.

5

Orlaya grandiflora
white laceflower

Clear white flowers in airy umbels are held on almost leafless stems.

annual
height 60cm (24in)
3 per m² (10ft²)
flowers from early summer to early autumn

Good for...

bumblebees
solitary bees
wasps
hoverflies
butterflies
moths
ladybirds
hibernating lacewing larvae

Be mine

The intention of this pocket planting is to capture the colours of high summer, matching richly coloured flowers with a bronze fennel chosen for its darkness and *Phlox drummondii* 'Cherry Caramel' in love-heart sweet hues. Dahlias first arrived in Georgian England from Mexico 200 years ago, and it was quickly discovered that they would produce a rich and varied offspring when crossed and grown from seed. *Dahlia* 'Soulman' is one of over 1,500 different cultivars listed today by the National Dahlia Collection and I like it for the petal-packed yet gently fading flowers. *Lilium* 'Stracciatella Event' is a tall lily with a good number of flowers and one bulb is enough to create an upper layer. The free-flowering annual *Phlox drummondii* 'Cherry Caramel' grows in a range of mutable hues.

Method

1 You can sow annual seeds in spring or in autumn. You will get earlier flowering and bigger plants if you sow in autumn and plant out in spring, after the frosts have gone.

2 Take a packet of *Phlox drummondii* 'Cherry Caramel' seed. Fill small pots with some seed compost, leaving a centimetre (half an inch) or so between the top of the compost and the rims of the pots for watering.

3 Tap each pot sharply on a flat surface to settle the compost and create a level surface for sowing. Sow the seed evenly, 5-10 seeds to a pot. Leave enough space between the seeds for the seedlings to germinate without crowding each other.

4 Leave the seeds uncovered and water carefully using a gentle flow of water. Label each pot and place it on a windowsill. Keep the compost damp and look for shoots pushing up in two to three weeks.

5 When the seedlings have their first true leaves - that is, the leaves of the plant itself rather than the 'seed leaves' which emerge first - transfer them to individual pots. Take care not to damage their delicate stems as you move them, holding each seedling by a leaf and supporting the weight of its roots. Put the seedlings on a windowsill to grow on until you are ready to plant them outside.

6 **In late winter** Use a spade to dig over the soil to a crumbly consistency, breaking up any big lumps.

7 Plant the *Lilium* 'Stracciatella Event' bulb, 10-15cm (4-6in) deep, with the pointy end facing upwards.

8 **In spring** Space the plants out on the soil in their pots, leaving enough room for each one to grow and fill out. Dahlias are particularly hungry plants, so add a spadeful of peat-free, general-purpose compost when you plant the *Dahlia* 'Soulman'.

9 Tap each plant from its pot and tease out some of the roots with your fingertips. Dig a hole for each plant to the same depth it was in its pot. Then plant and firm down the soil gently with your hands. Water all the plants thoroughly.

The 5 plants

1

Dahlia 'Soulman'

2

Dianthus barbatus 'Sweet Cherry Black'

3

Foeniculum vulgare 'Purpureum'

4

Lilium 'Stracciatella Event'

5

Phlox drummondii 'Cherry Caramel'

1

Dahlia 'Soulman'
dahlia

A luscious, plum-coloured, anemone-flowered dahlia with reflexed flowers.

perennial
height 1m (39in)
1 per m² (10ft²)
flowers from mid-summer to late summer

Note: Heap a spadeful of compost on top of the soil above the dahlia tubers to protect them during the coldest months, so that they return to flower the following year.

2

Dianthus barbatus 'Sweet Cherry Black'
sweet william

Fuzzy, green buds and flowers the colour of black cherries. Has a sweet scent.

perennial
height 30cm (12in)
1 per m² (10ft²)
flowers from early summer to late summer

3

Foeniculum vulgare 'Purpureum'
bronze fennel

Near-black, thread-like foliage and chartreuse, umbel flowers. Edible, from root to flower.

perennial
height 1.8m (6ft)
2 per m² (10ft²)
flowers from mid-summer to late summer

5

Phlox drummondii
'Cherry Caramel'
phlox

Soft mutable colours from a single
packet of seed. Bright scent.

annual
height 45cm (18in)
1 per m² (10ft²)
flowers from early summer to early autumn

4

Lilium 'Stracciatella Event'
lily

Clear white flowers with blackcurrant-
coloured centres and orange anthers.

bulb
height 1.2m (4ft)
1 per m² (10ft²)
flowers from early summer to mid-summer

Good for...

bumblebees
solitary bees
hoverflies
butterflies
shield bugs
ladybirds
hibernating lacewing larvae

This mid-summer combination plays with form and colour by using a glowing grass and the textural palette of emergent foliage as the foil for small, rich, dark flowers. *Cosmos atrosanguineus* - the chocolate cosmos - is native to Mexico and was once thought to be extinct in the wild. It is a good choice for a small garden, tucked against a sun-warmed wall where its chocolate scent can linger.

Hordeum jubatum is an enthusiastic self-seeder - one plant can quickly become many - so it's best confined to a small plot. *Actaea simplex* Atropurpurea Group has white, bottlebrush flowers in late summer.

The 5 plants

1

Actaea simplex Atropurpurea Group

2

Anaphalis triplinervis

3

Cosmos atrosanguineus

4

Hordeum jubatum

5

Sanguisorba 'Tanna'

Method

1 Use a spade to dig over the soil to a crumbly consistency, breaking up any big lumps.

2 Gather together all the plants.

3 Start by arranging the flowering plants - the *Cosmos atrosanguineus*, *Actaea simplex* Atropurpurea Group, *Anaphalis triplinervis* and *Sanguisorba* 'Tanna' - in their pots, spacing them out on the soil.

4 Thread the *Hordeum jubatum* grasses between the flowering plants. They will be a little sparse to begin with, but leave some space between them so they can knit together as they grow.

5 Tap each plant from its pot and tease out some of the roots with your fingertips. Dig a hole for each plant to the same depth it was in its pot, then plant and carefully firm down the soil with your hands.

6 Water all the plants thoroughly.

3

Cosmos atrosanguineus
chocolate cosmos

Small, velvety flowers on long stems. Distinct chocolate scent.

perennial
height 40cm (16in)
3 per m² (10ft²)
flowers from early summer to early autumn

1

Actaea simplex
Atropurpurea Group
baneberry

Tall stems with darkly hued leaves and spikes of white, bottlebrush flowers. Architectural seedheads in winter echo the shape of the former flowers.

perennial
height 1.5m (5ft)
1 per m² (10ft²)
flowers from early autumn to mid-autumn

2

Anaphalis triplinervis
everlasting

Papery, white flowers with greyish-green foliage and woolly stems.

perennial
height 70cm (28in)
2 per m² (10ft²)
flowers from mid-summer to late summer

4

Hordeum jubatum
foxtail barley

Pale, tuft-like flowers, recalling a field of barley, often tinged with red at the tips. An excitable self-seeder. Deciduous.

grass
height 60cm (24in)
2 per m² (10ft²)
flowers from early summer to early autumn

5

Sanguisorba 'Tanna'
burnet

A fuzz of bright ruby burrs bobbing on tall, wiry stems.

perennial
height 50cm (20in)
1 per m² (10ft²)
flowers from early summer to early autumn

Good for...

bumblebees
solitary bees
honeybees
hoverflies
butterflies
moths
hibernating ladybirds and lacewing larvae

This collection of pots is a deep dive into scent using flowers and leaves that smell good. Scented-leaf pelargoniums are grown for their fragrant leaves, and planted in an enclosed space, they will release their scent when you brush past. *Pelargonium* 'Mabel Grey' has bright lemony leaves and pale pink flowers that pair well with the deeply cut foliage of rose-scented *P.* 'Graveolens'. *P.* 'Chocolate Peppermint' adds deft colour, having warm pink flowers with deep cherry-red spots and a dark splodge to the middle of each leaf.

The bright, waxy leaves and white, starry flowers of a wall-trained jasmine, *Trachelospermum jasminoides*, have a sweet perfume in early summer.

Method

1 Fix galvanized wires horizontally to a wall, spacing them 20cm (8in) apart. Plant the *Trachelospermum jasminoides* at the foot of the wall, tilting the plant inwards. If there are any stems that will reach, thread them onto the lowest wires. Water thoroughly.

2 Choose four generously sized, clay pots as pelargoniums are fast-growing, hungry plants.

3 Cover the hole in the base of each pot with a pebble to keep the compost inside and pour in a good layer of horticultural grit to ensure sharp drainage.

4 Partially fill each pot with equal measures of peat-free, general-purpose compost and grit to create a beautifully open mix, leaving a centimetre (half an inch) or so between the top of the compost and the rim for watering.

5 Tap each *Pelargonium* out of its pot and loosen a few of the roots with your fingertips before digging a hole and planting one in each pot. Firm in gently and add more compost if necessary to fill any gaps. Water thoroughly.

6 Plants grown in pots need considerably more watering than those in the soil, so water daily at the height of summer.

Note: Plant this combination near a window and the scent will fill the house on warm days.

The 5 plants

1

Pelargonium 'Brilliantine'

2

Pelargonium 'Chocolate Peppermint'

3

Pelargonium 'Graveolens'

4

Pelargonium 'Mabel Grey'

5

Trachelospermum jasminoides

2

Pelargonium 'Chocolate Peppermint'
scented pelargonium

Chocolate-mint-scented leaves and pretty, middling-pink flowers with darker spots.

perennial
height 40cm (16in)
1 per pot
flowers from mid-summer to mid-autumn

3

Pelargonium 'Graveolens'
rose-scented pelargonium

Deeply cut, rose-scented leaves and small, bright, rosy flowers.

perennial
height 40cm (16in)
1 per pot
flowers from mid-summer to mid-autumn

1

Pelargonium 'Brilliantine'
scented pelargonium

Grey, scallop-edged leaves with a spicy scent. Tiny, pale flowers.

perennial
height 40cm (16in)
1 per pot
flowers from mid-summer to mid-autumn

5

Trachelospermum jasminoides
star jasmine

Brilliant white, star-shaped flowers with a deep, honey scent. Evergreen.

climber
height 9m (30ft)
1 only
flowers from early summer to late summer

4

Pelargonium 'Mabel Grey'
scented pelargonium

Bright, sherbet-scented leaves and small, pink flowers.

perennial
height 40cm (16in)
1 per pot
flowers from mid-summer to mid-autumn

Good for...

bumblebees
solitary bees
hoverflies
butterflies
moths

It is possible to grow things to eat even in a very small garden, but it is a good idea to choose edibles that are more difficult to buy. The sherbet-scented leaves of *Aloysia citrodora*, or lemon verbena, add a brightness to custards; *Ocimum basilicum* 'Mrs Burns' Lemon' makes a gin basil smash with a twist; a few leaves picked from *Pelargonium* 'Attar of Roses' can be used to rose-infuse a summer pudding. The list goes on.

I decided to plant my edible plants in a metal tub, choosing five plants that enjoy the same sunny conditions, compost and watering routine. They also all respond well to picking, which is essential in helping them to fill out.

Try to select a container that sets off the plants to good effect. A grey patina works beautifully with the chalky leaves of the heat-favouring plants.

The 5 plants

1
Aloysia citrodora

Method

1 **For the lemon basil** Fill a small pot with some seed compost, leaving a centimetre (half an inch) or so between the top of the compost and the rim for watering.

2 Tap the pot sharply on a flat surface to settle the compost and create a level surface for sowing. Sow 10-15 seeds, spacing them evenly and leaving enough room between them for the seedlings to grow without crowding each other.

3 Cover the seeds with a little more compost, and water it carefully, taking care not to dislodge the seeds. Label each pot and place it on a windowsill. Keep the compost damp. The seedlings will push up within seven days.

4 **To plant** Choose a tub with a good depth and drill some drainage holes in the base if there aren't some already. Cover each hole with a pebble to keep the compost inside.

5 Pour in a generous layer of horticultural grit for sharp drainage.

6 Mix together peat-free, general-purpose compost and grit in equal amounts, then fill the tub, leaving a centimetre (half an inch) or so between the top of the compost and the rim for watering.

7 Start with the tallest plants - the *Rosmarinus officinalis* 'Miss Jessopp's Upright' and *Aloysia citrodora*. Tap each plant from its pot and tease out a few of the roots with your fingertips. Scoop out holes towards the back of the tub and plant each one at the same depth it was in its pot. Scoop out two further holes at the front of the tub for the *Pelargonium* 'Attar of Roses' and the *Salvia officinalis*, taking them out of their pots and tucking them in.

8 Plant the *Ocimum basilicum* 'Mrs Burns' Lemon' in between the *Pelargonium* and the *Salvia*, keeping the small plants together as one. Fill any gaps between the plants with more compost and water the tub thoroughly.

Note: To pick, pinch off the tips of the shoots to encourage new ones to grow.

2
Ocimum basilicum 'Mrs Burns' Lemon'

3
Pelargonium 'Attar of Roses'

4
Rosmarinus officinalis 'Miss Jessopp's Upright'

5
Salvia officinalis

3

Pelargonium
'Attar of Roses'
rose-scented
pelargonium

Scalloped, grey-
green leaves
and pale rose-
pink flowers. An
enthusiastic grower.
Rose scent.

perennial
height 45cm (18in)
1 per pot
flowers from
early summer
to late autumn

2

Ocimum basilicum 'Mrs Burns'
Lemon'
basil

Basil, but with a lemony note.
Easily grown from seed.

annual
height 60cm (24in)
1 per pot
flowers from mid-summer to late summer

1

Aloysia citrodora
lemon verbena

A tall plant with pointed leaves and dainty,
white or pale lilac flowers. Useful for
adding height. Sherbet scent.

perennial
height 2.5m (8ft)
1 per pot
flowers from mid-summer to late summer

4

Rosmarinus officinalis 'Miss Jessopp's Upright'
rosemary

Dark green, needle-like leaves and vivid blue flowers. Aromatic evergreen.

shrub
height 2m (6½ft)
1 per pot
flowers from late spring to early summer

5

Salvia officinalis
common sage

Big, felty, grey-green leaves and spires of violet flowers.

perennial
height 1m (39in)
1 per pot
flowers from late spring to mid-summer

Good for...

bumblebees
solitary bees
honeybees
hoverflies
butterflies
moths

A brilliance of colour makes this planting scheme vibrate with energy. Bold, colourful and long-flowering perennials are often paired with grasses, and here *Dianthus carthusianorum*, *Salvia nemorosa* 'Amethyst' and *Veronicastrum virginicum* 'Lavendelturm' are woven together with the bee-like seedheads and narrow foliage of the grass *Briza media*. *Allium sphaerocephalon* is a reliably perennial bulb, which makes it a good choice for layered planting.

Once the flowers have had their time, the *Salvia nemorosa* 'Amethyst' and also the *Veronicastrum virginicum* 'Lavendelturm' will evolve in winter into seedheads that echo the shapes of the former flowers.

Method

1 Use a spade to dig over the soil to a crumbly consistency, breaking up any big lumps.

2 Gather together all the plants.

3 Stand all the plants on the soil, still in their pots, arranging like with like. All new planting looks a little sparse to begin with, but leave some space between the plants so they can knit together as they grow.

4 Tap each plant from its pot and tease out a few of the roots using your fingertips. Dig a hole for each plant to the same depth it was in its pot, then plant and firm down the soil gently with your hands.

5 Water all the plants thoroughly.

6 It is best to grow *Allium sphaerocephalon* in autumn from dormant bulbs to flower the following year. Bury the bulbs 10-15cm (4-6in) deep and with their pointy ends facing upwards, tucking them between the other plants. You can also buy them as budding bulbs in early summer, if you prefer.

Note: When new, green shoots push up though the soil in spring, use a pair of secateurs to cut back all the plants to soil level, ready to repeat the flowering cycle.

The 5 plants

1

Allium sphaerocephalon

2

Briza media

3

Dianthus carthusianorum

4

Salvia nemorosa 'Amethyst'

5

Veronicastrum virginicum 'Lavendelturm'

1

Allium sphaerocephalon
round-headed allium

Round, blackcurrant-coloured flowers atop straight, green stems and skinny foliage.

bulb
height 90cm (36in)
8 per m² (10ft²)
flowers from mid-summer to late summer

2

Briza media
lesser quaking grass

Bright green leaves and fat buds suspended in the air like a swarm of bees. Also has tiny, white flowers. Semi-evergreen.

grass
height 50cm (20in)
1 per m² (10ft²)
flowers from late spring to mid-summer

3

Dianthus carthusianorum
Carthusian pink

Small, intensely carmine flowers atop narrow stems. Subtle scent. Flowers for ages.

perennial
height 50cm (20in)
1 per m² (10ft²)
flowers from early summer to early autumn

4

Salvia nemorosa
'Amethyst'
Balkan clary

Upright spikes of
deep violet flowers.
Jam-packed with
pollen and nectar.

perennial
height 60cm (24in)
2 per m² (10ft²)
*flowers from
mid-summer to
early autumn*

5

Veronicastrum virginicum
'Lavendelturm'
Culver's root

Tall, vertical spikes whorled with tiny,
violet flowers. The flowers open on
consecutive days, offering pollinators lots
of opportunities to visit. Architectural
seedheads in winter.

perennial
height 1.5m (5ft)
2 per m² (10ft²)
flowers from mid-summer to early autumn

Good for...

bumblebees
solitary bees
honeybees
hoverflies
butterflies
ladybirds
hibernating lacewing larvae

This planting scheme is inspired by Wildside, the exciting, pioneering garden of plantsman Keith Wiley. Wildside takes its cue from plant communities worldwide, reconsidering them in the context of a garden.

Here, a tawny mini-savanna of *Stipa tenuissima* and *Eragrostis curvula* grasses intensifies the saturated colour of *Hemerocallis* 'Stafford' along with Quink-ink *Agapanthus* 'New Blue' and a pale *Campanula lactiflora*. *Hemerocallis* - the daylily - opens each of its flowers for just 24 hours, but in huge numbers and over a long period of time.

Form as well as colour is a useful tool in a small space, and the verticality of the grasses is a good foil to the flowers' more dynamic blooms.

The 5 plants

1

Agapanthus 'New Blue'

2

Campanula lactiflora

Method

1 Use a spade to dig over the soil to a crumbly consistency, breaking up any big lumps.

2 Gather together all the plants.

3 Starting with the *Hemerocallis* 'Stafford', *Agapanthus* 'New Blue' and *Campanula lactiflora*, space the plants out on the soil, still in their pots.

4 Thread the *Stipa tenuissima* and *Eragrostis curvula* between the first three plants, keeping in mind that the *Hemerocallis* and *Agapanthus* will eventually grow into quite chunky plants.

5 Tap each plant from its pot and tease out a few of the roots with your fingertips. Dig a hole for each plant to the same depth it was in its pot, before planting and firming down the soil carefully with your hands.

6 Water all the plants thoroughly.

Note: You can pinch off the flowers of the *Hemerocallis* once they have had their time.

3

Eragrostis curvula

4

Hemerocallis 'Stafford'

5

Stipa tenuissima

1

Agapanthus
'New Blue'
African lily

Umbels of inky
blue flowers with a
darker stripe down
the centre of each
petal. *Agapanthus*
grows well between
other plants.

perennial
height 80cm (32in)
1 per m² (10ft²)
*flowers from
mid-summer
to late summer*

2

Campanula lactiflora
milky bellflower

Sky-blue flower panicles on an airy plant.

perennial
height 1m (39in)
1 per m² (10ft²)
flowers from mid-summer to early autumn

3

*Eragrostis
curvula*
African love grass

A short, deciduous
grass topped with
tawny flowers in
autumn. Papery,
architectural
winter seedheads.

grass
height 90cm (36in)
3 per m² (10ft²)
*flowers from
early autumn to
mid-autumn*

4

Hemerocallis 'Stafford'
daylily

Strappy leaves and large, vermillion flowers
that each last for only one day. A robust
perennial that provides splashes of colour
between other plants.

perennial
height 80cm (32in)
1 per m² (10ft²)
flowers from mid-summer to late summer

5

Stipa tenuissima
**Mexican feather
grass**

A short, semi-
evergreen grass
with very fine,
green leaves. Turns
papery in autumn.

grass
height 40cm (16in)
3 per m² (10ft²)
*flowers from
early summer to
early autumn*

Good for...

bumblebees
solitary bees
honeybees
hoverflies
ladybirds
hibernating lacewing larvae

Echinacea pallida is one of my favourite flowers, having a tall, skinny stem and narrow, rippling flowers. It is a native plant of the North American prairies where it towers above other flowers with the intention of being the first flower to catch the attention of pollinators as they fly past, resulting in its good height. Here, it is matched with plants that have airy silhouettes, including *Verbena bonariensis, Perovskia atriplicifolia* 'Blue Spire' and *Eryngium* × *tripartitum*, which turns a more intense blue as summer progresses, offering high notes of intense colour.

The 5 plants

Method

1 Use a spade to dig over the soil to a crumbly consistency, breaking up any big lumps.

2 Gather together all the plants.

3 Arrange the plants in their pots on the soil, keeping like with like. All new planting looks a little sparse to begin with, but leave some space between the plants, so they can knit together as they grow.

4 Tap each plant from its pot and ease out some of the roots with your fingertips. Dig a hole for each plant to the same depth it was in its pot, then plant and firm down the soil carefully with your hands.

5 Water all the plants thoroughly.

6 When new, green shoots push up though the soil in spring, use a pair of secateurs to cut back all the plants to soil level ready to repeat the flowering cycle.

Note: Echinacea pallida, Eryngium × *tripartitum* and *Perovskia atriplicifolia* 'Blue Spire' all have architectural seedheads that will last throughout the cold winter months.

1
Echinacea pallida

2
Eryngium × *tripartitum*

3
Perovskia atriplicifolia 'Blue Spire'

4
Salvia nemorosa 'Caradonna'

5
Verbena bonariensis

1

Echinacea pallida
coneflower

Daisy-like flowers with narrow petals in palest pink with burnt orange centres. This gently self-sows in the garden and its seedlings are 'true' (identical to the original plant). Architectural seedheads in winter.

perennial
height 1.2m (4ft)
2 per m² (10ft²)
flowers from mid-summer to late autumn

2

Eryngium × tripartitum
sea holly, tripartite eryngo

Electric-blue thistle flowers inside sharp bracts and jagged leaves with sharp 'teeth'. The flowers turn more deeply blue as summer progresses. Architectural seedheads in winter.

perennial
height 70cm (28in)
2 per m² (10ft²)
flowers from late summer to mid-autumn

3

Perovskia atriplicifolia 'Blue Spire'
Russian sage

Velvety, blue buds and tiny, trumpet-like flowers on white stems. Has a warm, spicy scent.

perennial
height 1m (39in)
1 per m² (10ft²)
flowers from mid-summer to mid-autumn

4

Salvia nemorosa 'Caradonna'
Balkan clary

Upright spikes of inky flowers dotted on near-black stems. Jam-packed with pollen and nectar.

perennial
height 60cm (24in)
3 per m² (10ft²)
flowers from early summer to mid-autumn

5

Verbena bonariensis
verbena

Small, violet-blue flowers held at the tips of long, skinny stems. Useful for adding height in a small space. Easily grown from seed, if you wish.

perennial
height 2m (6½ft)
2 per m² (10ft²)
flowers from late spring to early autumn

Good for...

bumblebees
solitary bees
honeybees
hoverflies
butterflies
moths
hibernating ladybirds and lacewing larvae

A stylized version of nature, this design scheme works well in an urban space; the looseness of the planting juxtaposes with straight lines, rough surfaces and brick.

Dianthus carthusianorum, the intensely coloured Carthusian pink, has narrow stems and leaves that thread easily through *Stipa tenuissima* and *Briza media* grasses. Umbels are the predominant flower shape in nature and the dusky plum flowers of *Astrantia major* 'Star of Beauty' are picked up by the neon-violet spikes of *Liatris spicata* 'Kobold'. None of the plants is a huge spreader, so plant them almost as closely as you want in the finished pot.

Method

1 Choose a square or rectangular planter to contrast with the airiness of the plants. Drill drainage holes in the base, if there aren't some already. Cover the holes with a pebble to keep the compost inside.

2 Tip a few scoops of horticultural grit into the base of the planter to ensure sharp drainage and fill it with peat-free, general-purpose compost, leaving a centimetre (half an inch) or so between the compost and the rim for watering.

3 Gather together all the plants. Tap each plant from its pot and loosen a few of the roots with your fingertips.

4 Starting with the taller plants, position them in the planter, one by one. What is important here is the balance of the composition, with the narrow uprights emerging from the lower filler plants. The spaces between the plants are just as important as the plants themselves.

5 Scoop out a hole for each plant to the same depth it was in its pot, then plant and gently firm in. Fill any gaps between the plants with more compost. Water thoroughly.

6 If you wish, you can grow *Liatris spicata* 'Kobold' by planting the corms, 12cm (5in) deep, in small pots, ready to transfer as they come into leaf. The corms will need to have been planted in the preceding autumn to spend the winter in the cold and dark ready to flower in early summer.

The 5 plants

1

Astrantia major 'Star of Beauty'

2

Briza media

3

Dianthus carthusianorum

4

Liatris spicata 'Kobold'

5

Stipa tenuissima

1

Astrantia major 'Star of Beauty'
Hattie's pincushion

Papery flowers in a dusty plum colour with delicate seedheads that last all winter. *Astra* translates from the Latin as 'star', reflecting the shape of the flowers. Architectural seedheads in winter.

perennial
height 60cm (24in)
1 per pot
flowers from late spring to early autumn

2

Briza media
lesser quaking grass

Bright green leaves and big buds suspended in the air like a swarm of bees. Minuscule, white flowers. Semi-evergreen.

grass
height 50cm (20in)
1 per pot
flowers from late spring to mid-summer

3

Dianthus carthusianorum
Carthusian pink

Small, intensely carmine flowers atop narrow stems. Subtle scent. Flowers for ages.

perennial
height 50cm (20in)
1 per pot
flowers from early summer to early autumn

5

Stipa tenuissima
Mexican feather grass

A short, clump-forming, semi-evergreen grass with very fine, green leaves. Turns papery in autumn.

grass
height 40cm (16in)
2 per pot
flowers from early summer to early autumn

4

Liatris spicata 'Kobold'
blazing star

Neon-violet flowers on straight stems, each with a quirky line. Architectural seedheads in winter.

perennial
height 50cm (20in)
1 per pot
flowers from early summer to late summer

Good for...

bumblebees
solitary bees
honeybees
hoverflies
butterflies
ladybirds
hibernating lacewing larvae

A thoughtfully planted container is a good idea where soil space is limited. Pinpricks of intense colour from the flowering tips of the *Verbena officinalis* var. *grandiflora* 'Bampton' are picked up in the warm tones of *Origanum vulgare* and the tall, violet flowers of *Lobelia* × *speciosa* 'Tania'. A grass, *Carex testacea*, provides a good foil for the more colourful plants. This wide tub encourages the plants to mingle as they grow, as well as offering a good depth of compost. Plants growing in a container are at your mercy with regard to watering, so one big pot rather than several smaller ones is more forgiving, should you forget.

Method

1 Choose a good-sized container with holes in the base. Drill some drainage holes in the base, if there aren't some already. This wide, verdigris tub pairs well with the chalky tones of the plants.

2 Position the container where you want it to go before you start, as once filled with compost and planted it will be heavy and difficult to move.

3 Place a pebble over each hole to keep the compost inside, then fill the container with peat-free, general-purpose compost, leaving a centimetre (half an inch) or so between the top of the compost and the rim for watering.

4 These plants all grow swiftly within the space of one season, so start with the smallest plants you can find. Plant the *Carex testacea* first to provide the base note. Tap it out of its pot and loosen a few of the roots with your fingertips. Dig a hole and plant to the same depth it was in its pot, then carefully firm in with your hands.

5 Repeat this process with the *Verbena officinalis* var. *grandiflora* 'Bampton' and *Lobelia* × *speciosa* 'Tania', allowing the plants to thread together at their edges.

6 Position the low-growing plants, the *Origanum vulgare* and *Thymus vulgaris*, at the front to blur the edge of the container. Add more compost to fill any gaps between the plants, then water thoroughly.

Note: The verbena's dusky flowers glow in the evening light.

The 5 plants

1

Carex testacea

2

Lobelia × *speciosa* 'Tania'

3

Origanum vulgare

4

Thymus vulgaris

5

Verbena officinalis var. *grandiflora* 'Bampton'

3

Origanum vulgare
oregano

Pale corymbs of tiny flowers that are tinged with plum. Crush the leaves and they smell of hay, menthol and spice.

perennial
height 60cm (24in)
1 per pot
flowers from early summer to early autumn

1

Carex testacea
New Zealand sedge

A waxy, olive-green sedge with small flowers followed by black seedheads.

perennial
height 45cm (18in)
1 per pot
flowers from mid-summer to late summer, but usually grown for its foliage

2

Lobelia × speciosa 'Tania'
lobelia

Tall spikes of day-glow flowers on darkly coloured stems. The flowers open sequentially from base to tip, offering pollinators plenty of opportunities to visit.

perennial
height 90cm (36in)
1 per pot
flowers from early summer to early autumn

4

Thymus
vulgaris
common thyme

An edible herb with
green leaves and
tiny, pink flowers.
Camphor scent.

perennial
height 20cm (8in)
2 per pot
flowers from late
spring to mid-
summer

5

Verbena officinalis var.
grandiflora 'Bampton'
vervain

Tiny, violet-pink flowers at the tips of
arching stems that glow in the evening
light. Leaves serrated and tinged with plum.

perennial
height 1m (39in)
1 per pot
flowers from early summer to mid-autumn

Good for...

bumblebees
solitary bees
honeybees
bee-flies
hoverflies
butterflies
moths
ladybirds

Katy Merrington is the cultural gardener at Hepworth Wakefield Garden, in West Yorkshire, England, a public garden that is open 24 hours a day, 365 days a year. Central to the garden's design, by Tom Stuart-Smith, is the premise that our attachment to nature is made stronger with variety, and so the planting has been designed to evolve constantly throughout the year. A garden that works all year round is even more important in a smaller space where the plants can be seen every day, including through the windows of the home in winter.

In this planting scheme, the quirky lines and top-down flowers of *Liatris pycnostachya* combine with spiky, architectural, flat-topped *Achillea filipendulina* 'Gold Plate', colourful *Origanum laevigatum* 'Herrenhausen' and the blue flowers of *Perovskia atriplicifolia* 'Blue Spire' in a kaleidoscope of colour. In winter, the plants are beautiful in form and outline when the seedheads echo the shapes of the flowers.

The 5 plants

1
Achillea filipendulina 'Gold Plate'

2
Eryngium yuccifolium

3
Liatris pycnostachya

4
Origanum laevigatum 'Herrenhausen'

5
Perovskia atriplicifolia 'Blue Spire'

Method

1 Use a spade to dig over the soil to a crumbly consistency, breaking up any big lumps.

2 Gather together all the plants.

3 Arrange the plants on the soil, still in their pots, keeping like with like. All new planting looks a little sparse to begin with, but leave some space between the plants and they will knit together as they grow.

4 Take each plant out of its pot and loosen some of the roots using your fingertips. Dig a hole for each plant to the same depth it was in its pot before planting and carefully firming down the soil.

5 Water all the plants thoroughly.

Note: When new, green shoots push up through the soil in spring, use a pair of secateurs to cut back all the plants to soil level to repeat the flowering cycle.

1

Achillea filipendulina 'Gold Plate'
yarrow

Yellow, flat-headed flowers atop feathery foliage. Architectural seedheads in winter.

perennial
height 80cm (32in)
3 per m² (10ft²)
flowers from early summer to late summer

2

Eryngium yuccifolium
sea holly

Thistle flowers and sharp, jagged, green foliage. Architectural seedheads in the winter.

perennial
height 1.2m (4ft)
3 per m² (10ft²)
flowers from early summer to late summer

3

Liatris pycnostachya
blazing star

Neon-purple flowers on straight stems, each with a quirky line. Architectural seedheads in winter.

perennial
height 1.5m (5ft)
4 per m² (10ft²)
flowers from early summer to late summer

5

Perovskia atriplicifolia 'Blue Spire'
Russian sage

Velvety, blue buds and tiny, trumpet-like flowers held on white stems. Warm and spicily scented.

perennial
height 1m (39in)
1 m² (10ft²)
flowers from mid-summer to mid-autumn

4

Origanum laevigatum
'Herrenhausen'
oregano

Pale corymbs of small, rose-coloured flowers tinged with plum. Crush the leaves and they smell of hay, menthol and spice.

perennial
height 60cm (24in)
4 per m² (10ft²)
flowers from early summer to early autumn

Good for...

bumblebees
solitary bees
honeybees
hoverflies
butterflies
ladybirds
hibernating lacewing larvae

Mary Keen's mesmerizing small garden has been informed by a lifetime spent growing and observing plants. Her salvias are the most electric of blues; her dahlias the most luminous. Every plant has been carefully chosen as the very best there is. Here, the vibrant hollyhock, *Alcea rosea* 'Giant Single Mixed', provides an upper storey to *Erigeron annuus*, a fast- and free-flowering, daisy-like perennial that grows well between other robust perennial plants. This design requires a bit of planning, as hollyhocks are best grown from seed to avoid the murkier flower colours. Sow the seed on the surface of a tray of seed compost and select the seedlings with the darkest stems, which will grow on to have the most richly hued flowers.

Method

1   Take a packet of *Alcea rosea* 'Giant Single Mixed' seed. Sow the seed in spring or in autumn. You will get earlier flowering and bigger plants from an autumn sowing and spring planting, after the frosts have gone.

2   Fill a seed tray with some seed compost, tamping it down with your hands. Water the compost and sow a good number of seeds on the surface, spacing them widely. There is no need to cover the seeds with more compost. Put the seed tray somewhere warm, like a sunny windowsill. Keep the soil damp. The seeds will germinate in seven to ten days.

3   Once you see the first true leaves - that is, the leaves of the plant itself rather than the initial 'seed leaves' - move the seedlings with the darkest stems to individual pots. Take care not to damage the delicate stems as you move them, holding each seedling by a leaf and supporting the weight of the roots. Put the seedlings on a windowsill to grow on until you are ready to plant them.

4   **In spring** Use a spade to dig over the soil to a crumbly consistency, breaking up any big lumps. Start with the *Dahlia* 'Karma Fuchsiana' and *D.* 'Winston Churchill', spacing them out quite widely, as Dahlias grow into hefty plants. Dot the *Salvia patens* 'Giant form' between the dahlias in ones and, occasionally, twos. Repeat for the *Alcea*.

5   When you're happy with the composition, tap each plant from its pot and tease out some of the roots with your fingertips. Dig a hole for each plant to the same depth it was in its pot, then plant and firm down the soil gently with your hands.

6   Use the *Erigeron annuus* to fill the gaps between the other plants. Water thoroughly.

The 5 plants

1

Alcea rosea 'Giant Single Mixed'

2

Dahlia 'Karma Fuchsiana'

3

Dahlia 'Winston Churchill'

4

Erigeron annuus

5

Salvia patens 'Giant Form'

1

Alcea rosea 'Giant Single Mixed'
hollyhock

Tall spikes of open flowers in plum,
carmine and pink.

short-lived perennial
height 2m (6½ft)
1 per m² (10ft²)
flowers from early summer to early autumn

2

Dahlia 'Karma
Fuchsiana'
dahlia

Decorative dahlia
with warm pink
flowers that have
fluorescent, lime-
yellow centres.
A useful dahlia for
pollinators due to
the open flowers.

perennial
height 90cm (36in)
1 per m² (10ft²)
*flowers from
mid-summer
to early autumn*

3

Dahlia 'Winston Churchill'
dahlia

A smaller-flowered dahlia - in the Waterlily
category - with sharp pink blooms.

perennial
height 1.1m (3½ft)
1 per m² (10ft²)
flowers from mid-summer to early autumn

Note: Cutting the faded flowers of dahlias
will encourage new flowers to develop.

5

Salvia patens 'Giant Form'
sage

A tall salvia with felty leaves and luminous, blue flowers.

perennial
height 1m (39in)
2 per m² (10ft²)
flowers from mid-summer to mid-autumn

4

Erigeron annuus
tall fleabane

Daisy-like flowers with shiny, yellow centres. Quite short-lived, but makes itself more reliable by sowing itself about.

short-lived perennial
height 1m (39in)
3 per m² (10ft²)
flowers from mid-summer to early winter

Good for...

bumblebees
solitary bees
hoverflies
honeybees
butterflies
moths
ladybirds
hibernating lacewing larvae

Inspired by plantsman Jimi Blake's colourful and adventurous garden, Hunting Brook near Dublin, Ireland, plants with repeating shapes work together in this textural scheme. Spikes of *Agastache rugosa* 'Liquorice Blue' and *Nepeta racemosa* 'Walker's Low' match each other for height, punctuated by the tall and luminous spikes of *Lobelia × speciosa* 'Tania'. Tight, round *Xerochrysum bracteatum* 'Dragon Fire' creates a visual contrast in a rich deep plum. Using a limited palette of plants and repeating the same shapes works well in a small garden. It looks contemporary and lets the architectural shapes of the plants shine through.

Method

1 Use a spade to dig over the soil to a crumbly consistency, breaking up any big lumps.

2 Gather together all the plants.

3 Starting with the *Nepeta racemosa* 'Walker's Low', *Agastache rugosa* 'Liquorice Blue' and *Linaria vulgaris* 'Alba', stand the plants on the soil, still in their pots, in a loose, tessellating pattern.

4 Dot the *Lobelia × speciosa* 'Tania' here and there in an irregular pattern in between the *Nepeta*, *Agastache* and *Linaria*.

5 Next, add the *Xerochrysum bracteatum* 'Dragon Fire', again spacing the plants irregularly. Don't worry too much about finding an exact position for each plant, but try to imagine how they will look when they are fully grown - you are aiming for some ups and downs and repetitions.

6 Tap each plant from its pot and tease out some of the roots with your fingertips. Dig a hole for each plant to the same depth it was in its pot, then plant and firm down the soil gently with your hands.

7 Water all the plants thoroughly.

Note: Agastache rugosa 'Liquorice Blue' and *Xerochrysum bracteatum* 'Dragon Fire' both have beautiful architectural seedheads in winter.

The 5 plants

1

Agastache rugosa 'Liquorice Blue'

2

Linaria vulgaris 'Alba'

3

Lobelia × speciosa 'Tania'

4

Nepeta racemosa 'Walker's Low'

5

Xerochrysum bracteatum 'Dragon Fire'

1

Agastache rugosa 'Liquorice Blue'
giant hyssop

Chunky spikes of tiny, violet flowers crowded together on upright stems. Crush the leaves between your fingertips and they will smell of anise and mint. *Agastache* has arrow-shaped winter seedheads.

perennial
height 90cm (36in)
3 per m² (10ft²)
flowers from mid-summer to mid-autumn

2

Linaria vulgaris 'Alba'
toadflax

Lots of tiny, white, snapdragon flowers on gently curving stems. This is an annual plant that is straightforward to grow from seed.

annual
height 90cm (36in)
2 per m² (10ft²)
flowers from early summer to early autumn

3

Lobelia × *speciosa* 'Tania'
lobelia

Spikes of Day-Glow flowers on darkly coloured stems. The flowers open sequentially from base to tip, offering pollinators lots of chances to visit.

perennial
height 90cm (36in)
1 per m² (10ft²)
flowers from early summer to early autumn

4

Nepeta racemosa 'Walker's Low'
catmint

Lolling stems of small, trumpet-like
flowers that together look like a pointillist
painting. *Nepeta* is quite a lax plant, and
it will happily survive the odd flipflop or
Wellington boot if it spills onto the grass.
Citrus and spice scent.

perennial
height 60cm (24in)
3 per m² (10ft²)
flowers from early summer to mid-autumn

5

*Xerochrysum
bracteatum*
'Dragon Fire'
**strawflower,
everlasting flower**

Plum-coloured,
papery flowers with
a ruff of petal-like
bracts. Flowers that
last for months.

annual
height 1.2m (4ft)
2 per m² (10ft²)
*flowers from
mid-summer to
the first frosts*

Good for...

bumblebees
solitary bees (including the wool
carder bee)
honeybees
hoverflies
butterflies
hibernating ladybirds and lacewing larvae

This radicchio, blue and neon-pink scheme is from the garden of sheep farmer June Blake. A small but intensely planted garden, it is an ongoing experiment in colour. Near-black *Actaea simplex* Atropurpurea Group 'James Compton' is matched with a boisterous annual, *Atriplex hortensis* var. *rubra*, and together they are threaded with plants that look especially good against their darker leaves and stems. Annuals are a useful addition in a new garden. They flower constantly and quickly, and can be grown readily from seed in high numbers but at little cost. Most seed packets recommend sowing seed in spring, but you will get earlier flowering and bigger plants from an autumn sowing and spring planting. You can also buy annuals as small plants, rather than growing them from seed.

Method

1   Gather together packets of *Atriplex hortensis* var. *rubra* and *Cosmos bipinnatus* 'Xsenia' seeds. Fill small pots with some seed compost, leaving a centimetre (half an inch) or so between the top of the compost and the rims of the pots for watering.

2   Tap each pot sharply on a flat surface to settle the compost and create a level surface. Sow the seed evenly, 5-10 seeds per pot, leaving enough space for the seedlings to germinate without crowding. There is no need to cover the seeds with more compost. Water carefully with a gentle flow of water. Label each pot and place it on the windowsill. Keep the compost damp. The seedlings will appear in two or three weeks.

3   When the seedlings have their first true leaves - the true leaves of the plant rather than the 'seed leaves' - move to individual pots. Take care not to damage the delicate stems - hold each seedling by a leaf and support the roots. Put on a windowsill to grow on.

4   **In spring** Use a spade to dig the soil to a crumbly consistency, breaking up any lumps. First, arrange the *Actaea simplex* Atropurpurea Group 'James Compton' in their pots, then add the *Atriplex* in ones and twos, to make an irregular pattern. Dot the *Eryngium planum* between the *Actaea* and *Atriplex*, then weave in the *Cosmos*. Add the *Salvia* 'Trewithen Cerise' last.

5   Tap each plant out of its pot and loosen a few of the roots with your fingertips. Dig a hole for each plant to the same depth it was in its pot, then plant and firm in gently with your hands. Water all the plants thoroughly.

The 5 plants

1

Actaea simplex Atropurpurea Group 'James Compton'

2

Atriplex hortensis var. *rubra*

3

Cosmos bipinnatus 'Xsenia'

4

Eryngium planum

5

Salvia 'Trewithen Cerise'

1

Actaea simplex Atropurpurea Group 'James Compton'
baneberry

Tall stems with darkly hued leaves and spikes of white, bottlebrush flowers. Architectural seedheads in winter echo the shape of the former flowers.

perennial
height 1.5m (5ft)
1 per m² (10ft²)
flowers from early autumn to mid-autumn

2

Atriplex hortensis var. *rubra*
red mountain spinach, garden orache

Red-purple leaves and red, velveteen flowers. Easily grown from seed.

annual
height 1.2m (4ft)
2 per m² (10ft²)
flowers from mid-summer to late autumn, but usually grown for its foliage

3

Cosmos bipinnatus 'Xsenia'
cosmos

A tall annual with pink, daisy-like flowers that have yellow centres. Good in close company due to the threadlike foliage. Also easy to grow from seed.

annual
height 1.8m (6ft)
2 per m² (10ft²)
flowers from mid-summer to late summer

4

Eryngium planum
sea holly, blue eryngo

Metallic-blue, thimble flowers inside bracts and sharp, jagged leaves. Useful for pollinators, such as bumblebees.

perennial
height 70cm (28in)
2 per m² (10ft²)
flowers from early summer to late summer

5

Salvia 'Trewithen Cerise'
small-leaf sage

Upright spikes of neon-pink flowers on dark stems. Packed with pollen and nectar.

perennial
height 60cm (24in)
2 per m² (10ft²)
flowers from early summer to mid-autumn

Good for...

bumblebees
solitary bees
honeybees
hoverflies
butterflies
hibernating ladybirds and lacewing larvae

This container in deep, rusty red sits flat on the ground like a mound of soil. Its shape, colour and heft inspired me to plant it as a chance happening - the kind of spontaneous planting that I see growing at the foot of gateposts when I walk my dog each morning. *Dianthus superbus* has an enjoyably scrappy habit and here its rose-coloured tones are echoed by the colour of the *Tulbaghia violacea*. The grass *Stipa tenuissima* provides a background foil and the flowering plants in the display have leafless stems, which allows for a good density of planting. *Ranunculus acris* is an enlivening presence providing cheerful spots of brightest yellow.

The 5 plants

1
Dianthus superbus

Method

1 Gather together all the plants.

2 Choose a tub wider than it is tall, ideally in a natural material. None of these plants needs a long root run. Drill some drainage holes in the base of the tub, if there aren't some already.

2
Erigeron karvinskianus

3 Cover each hole in the base of the tub with a pebble and tip in a generous layer of horticultural grit.

4 Fill the tub with a peat-free, general-purpose compost, leaving a centimetre (half an inch) or so between the top of the compost and the rim for watering.

3
Ranunculus acris

5 Plant the grass, the *Stipa tenuissima*, first to provide a base note. Tap the plants out of their pots and loosen some of the roots with your fingertips. Dig a hole in the compost to the same depth the grasses were in their pots, spacing them out evenly, then plant and firm in gently with your hands.

6 Add the *Dianthus superbus* and *Tulbaghia violacea,* pushing the plants out of their pots from the underside to release them, teasing out some of the roots and tucking them in near the grasses.

4
Stipa tenuissima

7 Next add the *Ranunculus acris*, so that the long stems thread between the other plants. Finally, tuck the *Erigeron karvinskianus* around the edge of the tub.

8 Using your fingers, fill any gaps between the plants with compost. Water thoroughly.

5
Tulbaghia violacea

3

Ranunculus acris
meadow buttercup

A tall, graceful buttercup on a longer than average stem.

perennial
height 80cm (32in)
2 per pot
flowers from early summer to late summer

2

Erigeron karvinskianus
Mexican fleabane

Tight, green buds and dainty, daisy-like flowers. An excitable self-seeder.

perennial
height 20cm (8in)
2 per pot
flowers from late spring to mid-autumn

1

Dianthus superbus
fringed pink

Fringed, pink petals with deeper pink centres marked with green and narrow, grey-green foliage. Has a subtle scent.

perennial
height 40cm (16in)
2 per pot
flowers from late spring to late summer

4

Stipa tenuissima
Mexican feather grass

A clump-forming, semi-evergreen grass with very fine, green leaves. Turns papery in autumn.

grass
height 40cm (16in)
2 per pot
flowers from early summer to early autumn

5

Tulbaghia violacea
society garlic

Pale violet umbels of small, trumpet-like flowers. Super long-flowering and good for day- and night-flying pollinators.

perennial
height 50cm (20in)
2 per pot
flowers from early summer to early autumn

Good for...

bumblebees
solitary bees
honeybees
hoverflies
butterflies
moths
shield bugs
ladybirds
hibernating lacewing larvae

Saturated colours come into their own in autumn as the sun lowers in the sky. I like the warm bi-tones of *Digiplexis* 'Falcon Fire' and here it is matched with other deeply hued flowers. Dark, velvety *Cosmos atrosanguineus*, the chocolate cosmos, flowers from early summer until early autumn and its skinny stems knit together easily with nearby plants. The grass *Panicum virgatum* 'Rehbraun' adds volume and texture at height with its tiny, plum-toned flowers.

The 5 plants

Method

1 Use a spade to dig over the soil to a crumbly consistency, breaking up any big lumps.

2 Gather together all the plants.

3 Arrange the plants on the soil, still in their pots, keeping like with like. All new planting looks a little sparse to begin with, but leave some space between the plants so they can knit together as they grow.

4 Tap each plant from its pot and tease out some of the roots with your fingertips. Dig a hole for each plant to the same depth it was in its pot before planting and carefully firming down the soil with your hands.

5 Water all the plants thoroughly.

1

Cosmos atrosanguineus

2

Digiplexis 'Falcon Fire'

3

Helenium 'Kleine Aprikose'

4

Panicum virgatum 'Rehbraun'

5

Rudbeckia subtomentosa 'Henry Eilers'

1

Cosmos atrosanguineus
chocolate cosmos

Small, dark maroon, velvety flowers on long stems. Chocolate scent.

perennial
height 40cm (16in)
3 per m² (10ft²)
flowers from early summer to early autumn

2

Digiplexis 'Falcon Fire'
Canary Island foxglove

Dark, leafy foliage topped with tall spikes of tubular flowers. This is the cousin of the foxglove, but much longer flowering. Benefits from the microclimate of an enclosed city garden.

perennial
height 90cm (36in)
1 per m² (10ft²)
flowers from early summer to late autumn

3

Helenium 'Kleine Aprikose'
sneezeweed

Coppery yellow, daisy-like flowers with round, bobble centres. Black bobble seedheads in winter.

perennial
height 70cm (28in)
1 per m² (10ft²)
flowers from late summer to mid-autumn

5

Rudbeckia subtomentosa
'Henry Eilers'
coneflower

Daisy-like flowers with narrow, yellow petals and brown centres. Architectural seedheads in winter.

perennial
height 1.2m (4ft)
1 per m² (10ft²)
flowers from late summer to mid-autumn

4

Panicum virgatum 'Rehbraun'
switch grass

A deciduous, clump-forming grass with strappy foliage and airy flowers on ultra-thin stems. Architectural seedheads in winter.

grass
height 1.2m (4ft)
1 per m² (10ft²)
flowers from late summer to early autumn

Good for...

bumblebees
solitary bees
honeybees
hoverflies
butterflies
ladybirds
hibernating lacewing larvae

I am always drawn to blue flowers, and this plan takes its cue from inky blue *Salvia* 'Amistad'. A popular plant with garden designers, it is matched with sky-blue *Agastache* 'Blue Boa' and a milky-toned *Echinacea purpurea* 'White Swan'. *Salvia* 'Amistad' will flower continuously for six months. Once it has had its time, the dark blue calyces of the flowers continue the deep and dusky mood.

The 5 plants

1
Agastache 'Blue Boa'

2
Anemanthele lessoniana

3
Echinacea purpurea 'White Swan'

4
Rudbeckia fulgida var. *sullivantii* 'Goldsturm'

5
Salvia 'Amistad'

Method

1 Use a spade to dig over the soil to a crumbly consistency, breaking up any big lumps.

2 Arrange the plants on the soil, still in their pots, keeping like with like. All new planting will look a little sparse to begin with, but leave some space between the plants so they can knit together as they grow.

3 Tap each plant from its pot and tease out some of the roots with your fingertips. Dig a hole for each plant to the same depth it was in its pot before planting and carefully firming down the soil with your hands.

4 Water all the plants thoroughly.

Note: When new, green shoots push up though the soil in spring, use a pair of secateurs to cut back all the plants to soil level to repeat the flowering cycle.

1

Agastache 'Blue Boa'
giant hyssop

Spikes of sky-blue, bee-blue flowers. If you crush the leaves, they smell of lemon and liquorice. Has striking, arrow-shaped seedheads in winter.

perennial
height 60cm (24in)
2 per m² (10ft²)
flowers from mid-summer to mid-autumn

2

Anemanthele lessoniana
pheasant's tail grass

An evergreen grass with narrow, olive-green leaves that turn amber as the nights draw in.

grass
height 1m (39in)
3 per m² (10ft²)
flowers from early spring to early autumn, but usually grown for its foliage

3

Echinacea purpurea 'White Swan'
coneflower

A compact perennial that has pale, daisy-like flowers with dull yellow centres. Architectural seedheads follow in winter.

perennial
height 60cm (24in)
2 per m² (10ft²)
flowers from early summer to early autumn

4

Rudbeckia fulgida var. *sullivantii* 'Goldsturm'
black-eyed Susan

Glowing yellow, daisy-like flowers with black bobble centres followed by bobble seedheads in winter.

perennial
height 60cm (24in)
1 per m² (10ft²)
flowers from late summer to mid-autumn

5

Salvia 'Amistad'
sage

Tall, vertical spikes of inky-blue flowers with almost-black calyces. A popular plant with garden designers.

perennial
height 1.2m (4ft)
1 per m² (10ft²)
flowers from mid-summer to mid-autumn

Good for...

bumblebees
solitary bees
honeybees
hoverflies
lacewings
butterflies
hibernating ladybirds and lacewing larvae

Tulbaghia are one of my favourite perennials and this high/low combination uses two different types: *Tulbaghia violacea* and *Tulbaghia* 'Fairy Star'. *Tulbaghia* flower for ages, and in this planting scheme they are the constant note among a myriad of changing flowers. Their quasi-grassy foliage is repeated in *Deschampsia cespitosa* 'Goldtau', a grass with tawny pink flowers in early summer. In high summer, the flowers of *Anemone* WILD SWAN ('Macane001') have violet backs offering flashes of colour. *Actaea simplex* Atropurpureum Group 'James Compton', chosen for its foil of dark foliage, has bright bristles of flower in early autumn.

Method

1 Use a spade to dig over the soil to a crumbly consistency, breaking up any big lumps.

2 Gather together all the plants.

3 Start with the tall plants, the *Actaea simplex* Atropurpureum Group 'James Compton' and *Deschampsia cespitosa* 'Goldtau'. Arrange the plants on the soil, still in their pots, thinking about how tall each one will be once it is fully grown.

4 Working outwards, add the *Tulbaghia violacea* and *Tulbaghia* 'Fairy Star'.

5 Use the *Anemone* WILD SWAN ('Macane001') to fill the spaces between the *Actaea* and *Deschampsia*, aiming for some ups and downs.

6 Tap each plant from its pot and tease out some of the roots with your fingertips. Dig a hole for each plant to the same depth it was in its pot before planting and carefully firming down the soil with your hands.

7 Water all the plants thoroughly.

Note: Don't cut off the faded flower heads if you would like to enjoy the architectural seedheads in winter.

The 5 plants

1

Actaea simplex Atropurpureum Group 'James Compton'

2

Anemone WILD SWAN ('Macane001')

3

Deschampsia cespitosa 'Goldtau'

4

Tulbaghia 'Fairy Star'

5

Tulbaghia violacea

1

Actaea simplex Atropurpurea Group 'James Compton'
baneberry

Tall stems with plum-hued leaves and spikes of brilliant white, bottlebrush flowers. Architectural seedheads in winter that echo the shape of the former flowers.

perennial
height 1.5m (5ft)
2 per m² (10ft²)
flowers from early autumn to mid-autumn

2

Anemone WILD SWAN ('Macane001')
windflower

Mother-of-pearl flowers held high on tall stems. Happy to be buffeted by wind and rain. Cotton-wool seedheads in winter.

perennial
height 1-1.5m (3-5ft)
2 per m² (10ft²)
flowers from late summer to late autumn

3

Deschampsia cespitosa 'Goldtau'
tufted hair grass

Gauzy, evergreen grass with tiny, tawny pink flowers in early summer. Papery seedheads in winter.

grass
height 90cm (36in)
3 per m² (10ft²)
flowers from early summer to late summer

4
Tulbaghia
'Fairy Star'
society garlic

Small, pale pink flowers. Smaller than
the species *Tulbaghia violacea*, and also
a prolific flowerer.

perennial
height 40cm (16in)
2 per m² (10ft²)
flowers from early summer to early autumn

5
Tulbaghia
violacea
society garlic

Pale violet
umbels of small
flowers held in
'constellations'.
Long-flowering.

perennial
height 50cm (20in)
2 per m² (10ft²)
*flowers from early
summer to early
autumn*

Good for...

bumblebees
solitary bees
honeybees
hoverflies
butterflies
moths
useful material for nest builders

Due to environmental change, a gradual shift in weather patterns has led to hotter, drier summers and winters that are wet but not cold. As a consequence, the traditional go-to palette of an English flower garden - delphiniums, peonies and other blowsy flowers - is being reconsidered by forward-thinking garden designers such as Tom Stuart-Smith in favour of more climate-friendly plants.

Echinacea pallida, Euphorbia corollata, Liatrus spicata and the bobble flowers of *Eryngium yuccifolium* have the flowering brilliance of the traditional palette, but like 'scratchy' soil that doesn't hold on to winter wet and they don't need watering in the height of summer.

Method

1 Use a spade to dig over the soil to a crumbly consistency, breaking up any big lumps.

2 Gather together all the plants.

3 Start with the *Eryngium yuccifolium* and *Euphorbia corollata*, spacing out the plants on the soil, still in their pots, in groups of two and three. Allow the two species to thread together at their tips.

4 Next, add the *Symphyotrichum turbinellum* in an ad hoc way, again in small groups.

5 Finally, add the *Echinacea pallida* and *Liatrus spicata* in pairs and threes between the *Euphorbia* and *Symphyotrichum*. All new planting looks a little sparse to begin with, but the plants will knit together to cover the soil as they grow.

6 Tap each plant from its pot and tease out some of the roots with your fingertips. Dig a hole for each plant to the same depth it was in its pot, before planting and carefully firming down the soil with your hands.

7 Water all the plants thoroughly.

The 5 plants

1

Echinacea pallida

2

Eryngium yuccifolium

3

Euphorbia corollata

4

Liatrus spicata

5

Symphyotrichum turbinellum

1

Echinacea pallida
coneflower

Daisy-like flowers that have narrow petals in pale pink with burnt orange centres. Architectural seedheads follow in winter.

perennial
height 1.2m (4ft)
2 per m² (10ft²)
flowers from mid-summer to late autumn

2

Eryngium yuccifolium
rattlesnake master

Grey-blue, thistle flowers inside sharp bracts and jagged leaves with sharp 'teeth'. Architectural seedheads in winter.

perennial
height 1.2m (4ft)
2 per m² (10ft²)
flowers from mid-summer to mid-autumn

3

Euphorbia corollata
garden spurge

Narrow, forking stems, each tipped with a tiny, delicate, white flower.

perennial
height 80cm (32in)
1 per m² (10ft²)
flowers from mid-summer to early autumn

4

Liatrus spicata
blazing star

Tall, fuzzy, neon-
purple flowers.
Architectural
seedheads appear
in winter and echo
the shape of the
former flowers.

perennial
height 1m (39in)
3 per m² (10ft²)
*flowers from
mid-summer to
mid-autumn*

5

Symphyotrichum turbinellum
aster

Super-airy, violet, daisy-like flowers held
in a 'constellation' and each with a yellow
centre. Black stems. Sometimes known
as *Aster turbinellus*.

perennial
height 90cm (36in)
1 per m² (10ft²)
flowers from mid-summer to mid-autumn

Good for...

bumblebees
solitary bees
honeybees
hoverflies
butterflies
ladybirds
hibernating lacewing larvae

In the tiniest garden, height is everything. *Verbena bonariensis* is a tall plant with small, violet flowers held at the tips of a scaffold of skinny stems. It grows upwards, but takes up very little room in the soil. Matched here with a couple of grasses, the airy *Panicum virgatum* 'Northwind' and *Molinia caerulea* subsp. *caerulea* 'Heidebraut', and with a violet-blue colour pop from *Agastache* 'Blue Fortune', it should be considered an essential plant for the smallest spaces.

The 5 plants

1

Agastache 'Blue Fortune'

2

Hylotelephium 'Vera Jameson'

3

Molinia caerulea subsp. *caerulea* 'Heidebraut'

4

Panicum virgatum 'Northwind'

5

Verbena bonariensis

Method

1 Use a spade to dig over the soil to a crumbly consistency, breaking up any big lumps.

2 Gather together all the plants.

3 Arrange the plants on the soil, still in their pots, keeping like with like. All new planting looks a little sparse to begin with, but leave some space between the plants so they can knit together as they grow.

4 Tap each plant from its pot and tease out some of the roots with your fingertips. Dig a hole for each plant to the same depth it was in its pot before planting and carefully firming down the soil with your hands.

5 Water all the plants thoroughly.

Note: When new, green shoots push up though the soil in spring, use a pair of secateurs to cut back all the plants to soil level to repeat the flowering cycle.

3

Molinia caerulea subsp. *caerulea* 'Heidebraut'
purple moor grass

A robust, upright, deciduous grass. Its flower spikes are violet-tinted before turning pale as winter seedheads.

grass
height 1.1m (3½ft)
1 per m² (10ft²)
flowers from late summer to early autumn

2

Hylotelephium 'Vera Jameson'
stonecrop

A low-level succulent with dusky pink leaves and tiny, star-shaped flowers.

perennial
height 20cm (8in)
2 per m² (10ft²)
flowers from late summer to early autumn

1

Agastache 'Blue Fortune'
giant hyssop

Chunky spikes of tiny, violet-blue flowers crowded together on upright stems. Crush the leaves between your fingertips and they smell of peppermint. Arrow-shaped seedheads in winter.

perennial
height 90cm (36in)
1 per m² (10ft²)
flowers from mid-summer to mid-autumn

4

*Panicum
virgatum
'Northwind'*
switch grass

Clump-forming,
deciduous grass
with airy flowers
held on ultra-thin
stems. Architectural
winter seedheads.

grass
height 1.8m (6ft)
1 per m² (10ft²)
*flowers from
late summer
to early autumn*

5

Verbena bonariensis
verbena

Small, violet-blue flowers held at the tips of
long, skinny stems. Easily grown from seed,
if you wish.

perennial
height 2m (6½ft)
3 per m² (10ft²)
flowers from late spring to early autumn

Good for...

bumblebees
solitary bees
honeybees
hoverflies
butterflies
ladybirds
hibernating lacewing larvae

This textural scheme for a small, sunny garden is inspired by the work of garden designer Piet Oudolf. Piet's designs are usually attached to hip architectural buildings in some of the world's most notable locations, including Noma, in Copenhagen, and the High Line in New York. Piet celebrates plants at every stage in their lifecycle, from shoot to bud to flower to seedhead, and to be chosen plants must look as good in winter as they do in the first unfurling of spring. This planting design ticks all the boxes for early autumn - pattern, texture and colour - before the plants evolve into stylized versions of their former flowers.

The 5 plants

1

Actaea simplex 'Pink Spike'

Method

1 Use a spade to dig over the soil to a crumbly consistency, breaking up any big lumps.

2 Gather together all the plants.

3 Start with the *Molinia caerulea* subsp. *caerulea* 'Poul Petersen', spacing the plants out on the soil, still in their pots, in groups of two or three.

4 Add the *Actaea simplex* 'Pink Spike' next to the *Molinia*, so the plants can thread together as they grow.

5 Next, add the *Sanguisorba officinalis* 'Red Buttons' in between, again in pairs and also in small groups.

6 Here and there, among the *Sanguisorba*, add the *Dianthus carthusianorum* to provide some points of bright colour. Then add the *Persicaria amplexicaulis* 'Alba' in between the taller plants.

7 Tap each plant from its pot and tease out some of the roots with your fingertips. Dig a hole for each plant to the same depth it was in its pot before planting and carefully firming down the soil with your hands.

8 Water all the plants thoroughly.

Note: When new, green shoots push up though the soil in spring, use a pair of secateurs to cut back all the plants to soil level to repeat the flowering cycle.

2

Dianthus carthusianorum

3

Molinia caerulea subsp. *caerulea* 'Poul Petersen'

4

Persicaria amplexicaulis 'Alba'

5

Sanguisorba officinalis 'Red Buttons'

3

Molinia caerulea subsp. *caerulea* 'Poul Petersen'
purple moor grass

A robust, deciduous grass that is useful for supporting more lax plants. The flower spikes are darkly tinted before turning pale as seedheads.

grass
height 70cm (28in)
2 per m² (10ft²)
flowers from late summer to late autumn

1

Actaea simplex 'Pink Spike'
baneberry

Tall stems with plum-hued leaves and spikes of pale, bottlebrush flowers. Architectural seedheads in winter echo the shape of the former flowers.

perennial
height 1.5m (5ft)
2 per m² (10ft²)
flowers from early autumn to mid-autumn

2

Dianthus carthusianorum
Carthusian pink

Small, intensely carmine flowers atop straight, narrow stems. Flowers for ages. Subtle scent.

perennial
height 50cm (20in)
1 per m² (10ft²)
flowers from early summer to early autumn

4

*Persicaria
amplexicaulis*
'Alba'
bistort

A robust, leafy
perennial with tall,
tapering spikes of
small, pale flowers.

perennial
height 1.2m (4ft)
1 per m² (10ft²)
*flowers from
mid-summer
to mid-autumn*

5

Sanguisorba officinalis
'Red Buttons'
burnet

A fuzz of bright ruby burrs on tall,
wiry stems.

perennial
height 1.2m (4ft)
3 per m² (10ft²)
flowers from early summer to early autumn

Good for...

bumblebees
solitary bees
honeybees
hoverflies
butterflies
ladybirds
hibernating lacewing larvae

Roses start setting their hips in autumn as dark, glistening fruits that last throughout the coldest months. The wild rose, *Rosa glauca*, is one of the earliest roses to fruit, with scarlet hips on arching, cinnamon-coloured stems. Roses can be tricky in a small garden due to the transience of their flowers, but *R. glauca* is useful for its early foliage, which is pewter-coloured and offers a good background to earlier flowers. Its single, open blooms feel refreshing among more petal-packed flowers and are good news for pollinating insects. Here, the burnished brown grass *Pennisetum alopecuroides* 'Cassian's Choice' and the newly coppered foliage of *Gillenia trifolata* highlight the colour of the rosehips.

The 5 plants

1
Gillenia trifolata

2
Pennisetum alopecuroides 'Cassian's Choice'

3
Rosa glauca

4
Solidago × luteus 'Lemore'

5
Symphyotrichum oblongifolium 'October Skies'

Method

1 Use a spade to dig over the soil to a crumbly consistency, breaking up any big lumps.

2 Gather together all the plants.

3 It is useful to think of this planting composition in layers. Start with the tallest-growing plant, the *Rosa glauca*. Remove the rose from its pot and gently tease out some of the roots with your fingertips. Dig a hole to a good depth, then plant the rose and firm it in using a booted foot.

4 The *Gillenia trifolata* and *Symphyotrichum oblongifolium* 'October Skies' provide the foliage and flower layer. Tap the plants from their pots and loosen some of the roots with your fingertips before planting under the dappled canopy of the rose. Carefully firm the plants into the soil with your hands.

5 Next, plant the *Pennisetum alopecuroides* 'Cassian's Choice' and *Solidago × luteus* 'Lemore' at the edge of the composition where the light is less filtered.

6 Water all the plants thoroughly.

3

Rosa glauca
wild rose

Single, pink flowers
with yellow centres
followed by
brilliantly scarlet
hips. Benefits from
a long, cool root
run to fuel the plant
so it will flower
reliably and well.
Deciduous.

shrub
height 1.8m (6ft)
1 per m² (10ft²)
*flowers from early
summer to late
summer; hips from
early autumn to
mid-winter*

1

Gillenia trifolata
Bowman's root

Tiny, white, star-like flowers and green
foliage that turns copper in autumn.

perennial
height 90cm (36in)
1 per m² (10ft²)
flowers from early summer to late summer

2

Pennisetum alopecuroides
'Cassian's Choice'
Chinese fountain grass

A deciduous grass with grassy leaves and
burnished brown, bottlebrush flowers.

grass
height 1.2m (4ft)
2 per m² (10ft²)
flowers from mid-summer to early autumn

4

*Solidago ×
luteus* 'Lemore'
golden rod

Narrow leaves and
loose bunches of
pale lemon, daisy-
like flowers.

perennial
height 60cm (24in)
2 per m² (10ft²)
*flowers from
late summer
to early autumn*

5

Symphyotrichum oblongifolium
'October Skies'
small-flowered aster

Violet, daisy-like flowers with yellow
centres that are borne in good numbers.

perennial
height 60cm (24in)
1 per m² (10ft²)
flowers from late summer to early winter

Good for...

bumblebees
solitary bees
honeybees
hoverflies
butterflies
moths
birds
caterpillars
ladybirds
hibernating ladybirds

One of the loveliest attributes of subtle, pale plants is that they gleam as the light levels fall at dusk. This planting scheme uses a palette of grey, green and white in different textures and shapes. The round, silvery leaves of *Alchemilla mollis* contrast with the small flowers of *Astrantia major* 'Large White' and the perpendicular stems of the grass *Sesleria autumnalis*. *Hydrangea quercifolia* has supersized panicles of bright white flowers.

The 5 plants

___

1

Alchemilla mollis

___

2

Astrantia major 'Large White'

___

3

Hydrangea quercifolia

___

4

Miscanthus sinensis 'Morning Light'

___

5

Sesleria autumnalis

Method

1 Use a spade to dig over the soil to a crumbly consistency, breaking up any big lumps.

2 Gather together all the plants.

3 It is useful to think of this planting composition in layers. Start with the tallest-growing plant, the *Hydrangea quercifolia*. Remove the hydrangea from its pot and loosen some of the roots with your fingertips. Dig a hole to a good depth, then plant and firm in using a booted foot.

4 Arrange the grasses - the *Miscanthus sinensis* 'Morning Light' and *Sesleria autumnalis* - in their pots on the soil next, keeping like with like, followed by the *Alchemilla mollis* and *Astrantia major* 'Large White' as the base layer.

5 Tap all the plants from their pots and ease out some of the roots with your fingertips before planting and carefully firming into the soil with your hands.

6 Water all the plants thoroughly.

1

Alchemilla mollis
lady's mantle

Textural, serrated foliage and a haze of citrus-bright flowers.

perennial
height 60cm (24in)
2 per m² (10ft²)
flowers from early summer to early autumn

2

Astrantia major 'Large White'
Hattie's pincushion

White, papery umbels with green tips. *Astra* translates from the Latin as 'star', reflecting the shape of the flowers. Architectural seedheads follow in winter.

perennial
height 60cm (24in)
2 per m² (10ft²)
flowers from late spring to early autumn

3

Hydrangea quercifolia
oak-leaved hydrangea

Bright green leaves that are shaped like giant oak leaves and big, blowsy panicles of pale flowers. Deciduous.

shrub
height 2m (6½ft)
1 per m² (10ft²)
flowers from mid-summer to early autumn

5

Sesleria autumnalis
autumn moor grass

Ribbon-shaped leaves and tiny, papery
flowers. The delicate seedheads last all
winter long. Evergreen.

grass
height 1.2m (4ft)
2 per m² (10ft²)
flowers from early summer to mid-autumn

4

Miscanthus sinensis 'Morning Light'
silver grass

Pearled tassels of flowers and cotton-wool-
like seedheads. The leaves have narrow,
cream margins. Deciduous.

grass
height 1.8m (6ft)
1 per m² (10ft²)
flowers from late summer to mid-autumn

Good for...

bumblebees
solitary bees
honeybees
day- and night-flying moths
hibernating ladybirds

I put this planter together in early winter as the plants were starting into growth, to replicate the tessellating patterns of a woodland floor. The wide, shallow pan encourages you to look down on the composition from above, just as you might see the plants on a winter walk. *Helleborus × sahinii* 'Winterbells', chosen for the subtlety of its flowers, provides an upper storey to *Cyclamen hederifolium* in both variegated and non-variegated forms. I like the unassuming nature of the hovering flowers and in particular their foliage, which is either traced with silvered markings or pale and round. I've arranged the plants like-with-like in the planter to suggest the way the different species would clump together to colonize a woodland floor.

Method

1 Choose a wide, shallow pan and drill some holes in the base if there aren't some already. Cover each hole with a pebble to keep the compost inside.

2 Fill the pan with a good-quality, peat-free, general-purpose compost, leaving a centimetre (half an inch) or so between the top of the compost and the rim for watering.

3 Scoop out a planting hole in the compost that is slightly offset from the middle. Beginning with the tallest plant - the *Helleborus × sahinii* 'Winterbells' - take it from its pot and ease out a few of the roots using your fingertips. Then plant to the same depth it was in its pot and firm in gently with your hands.

4 Next, plant the *Cyclamen hederifolium* and *C. hederifolium* Silver-leaved Group, upturning each one into your open hand and letting the stems thread between your fingers to protect the flowers as you remove them from their pots. Dig a hole for each one, then plant and firm in, arranging them in species groups.

5 Add the heathers next - the *Erica × darleyensis* 'J. W. Porter' and *Erica × darleyensis* 'Kramer's Rote', planting them in the same way. Tuck some more compost between the plants to fill any gaps. Water thoroughly.

The 5 plants

1

Cyclamen hederifolium

2

Cyclamen hederifolium Silver-leaved Group

3

Erica × darleyensis 'J. W. Porter'

4

Erica × darleyensis 'Kramer's Rote'

5

Helleborus × sahinii 'Winterbells'

3

Erica ×
darleyensis
'J. W. Porter'
heather

Green, needle-like
leaves growing
on a low, woody,
evergreen plant.

perennial
height 25cm (10in)
2 per pot
flowers from
mid-winter to
late spring

2

Cyclamen hederifolium
Silver-leaved Group
ivy-leaved cyclamen

Dark green foliage with textural markings
and sweetly pink flowers.

bulb
height 15cm (6in)
2 per pot
flowers from mid-autumn to early winter

1

Cyclamen hederifolium
ivy-leaved cyclamen

Pale, round leaves that reflect the light and
hovering, pink flowers. The flower stems
corkscrew the seeds down to the soil after
the flowers fade.

bulb
height 15cm (6in)
2 per pot
flowers from mid-autumn to early winter

4

*Erica ×
darleyensis*
'Kramer's Rote'
heather

Deep green, needle-
like leaves growing
on a low, woody,
evergreen plant.

perennial
height 25cm (10in)
2 per pot
*flowers from
mid-winter to
late spring*

5

Helleborus × sahinii 'Winterbells'
hellebore

Pale, bell-like flowers under long-lasting,
architectural foliage.

perennial
height 50cm (20in)
1 per pot
flowers from early winter to mid-spring

Good for...

early bumblebee queens
solitary bees
hoverflies

In this planting scheme, umbrella umbels, flat-topped fennels, the knotty bumps of *Phlomis russeliana* on straight stems, quivering grasses and the bobble flowers of *Echinacea purpurea* 'White Swan' all evolve into architectural seedheads in winter. Considering what to plant for winter is even more important in a tiny garden where the space can be seen through the windows of the home. Post-bloom, these seedheads have become stylized versions of the former flowers.

You can plant a garden at any time of year provided the soil isn't frozen. Ideally, plant this scheme in early summer, so that the plants can knit together as they grow, but then leave the spent flowers in place, to allow you to enjoy their seedheads rimed in frost during the shortest, darkest days.

Method

1 Use a spade to dig over the soil to a crumbly consistency, breaking up any big lumps.

2 Gather together all the plants.

3 Start with the grasses, the *Miscanthus sinensis* and *Pennisetum alopecuroides* 'Cassian's Choice', then follow on with the *Phlomis russeliana* and *Echinacea purpurea* 'White Swan'. Arrange the plants on the soil, still in their pots, grouping them in twos or threes.

4 Dot the *Foeniculum vulgare* here and there to thread between the other plants.

5 Tap each plant from its pot and loosen some of the roots with your fingertips. Dig a hole for each plant to the same depth it was in its pot, then plant and carefully firm in the soil with your hands.

6 Water all the plants thoroughly.

7 When the weather and soil begin to warm up the following spring, look out for new, green shoots pushing up at the base of each plant. When these shoots reach 10-15cm (4-6in) in height, use a sharp pair of secateurs to cut off the old stems, leaving a brown stalk behind. You can repeat this each spring as the plants restart their annual cycle.

The 5 plants

1

Echinacea purpurea 'White Swan'

2

Foeniculum vulgare

3

Miscanthus sinensis

4

Pennisetum alopecuroides 'Cassian's Choice'

5

Phlomis russeliana

1

Echinacea
purpurea
'White Swan'
coneflower

Pale, daisy-like
flowers with yellow
centres that are
followed by dark
bobble seedheads.

perennial
height 60cm (24in)
1 per m² (10ft²)
flowers from
early summer
to early autumn;
seedheads from
mid-autumn
to late winter

2

Foeniculum vulgare
fennel

Feathery, bright green foliage and
chartreuse, umbel flowers. Edible,
from root to flower.

perennial
height 1.8m (6ft)
2 per m² (10ft²)
flowers from mid-summer to late summer;
seedheads from early autumn to late winter

3

Miscanthus
sinensis
silver grass

Pearled tassels
of flowers and
cotton-wool-
like seedheads.
Deciduous.

grass
height 1.8m (6ft)
1 per m² (10ft²)
flowers from
late summer to
mid-autumn;
seedheads from
late autumn
to early spring

4

Pennisetum alopecuroides
'Cassian's Choice'
Chinese fountain grass

Grassy leaves and burnished brown,
bottlebrush flowers and seedheads.
Deciduous.

grass
height 1.2m (4ft)
2 per m² (10ft²)
*flowers from mid-summer to early autumn;
seedheads from late autumn to late winter*

5

*Phlomis
russeliana*
phlomis

Butter-yellow
flowers and bobble
seedheads.

perennial
height 1.2m (4ft)
1 per m² (10ft²)
*flowers from
mid-summer to
late summer;
seedheads from
early autumn to
early spring*

Good for...

material for nest builders
seeds for birds
hibernating solitary bees, ladybirds
and lacewing larvae

To the uninitiated, a snowdrop is just a snowdrop, but to a galanthophile differences in the minutiae of their markings, the configuration of their petals and the nuances of colour, combined with the fact that they flower when little else does, have made them a collector's flower. As a result, a single bulb of a rare or unusual snowdrop can sell for over £1,000. A starter collection of snowdrops in individual clay pots encourages an appreciation of the delicacy and beauty of their flowers. Snowdrops are best planted as dormant bulbs in autumn. A layer of moss from a sustainable source helps to keep their roots cool and stops the flowers getting splashed when it rains. This collection uses five different snowdrops, but more or fewer would be just as effective.

The 5 plants

1

Galanthus nivalis 'Anna Mill'

2

Galanthus plicatus 'Bryan Hewitt'

3

Galanthus plicatus 'Joe Sharman'

4

Galanthus plicatus 'Sarah Dumont'

5

Galanthus woronowii 'Elizabeth Harrison'

Method

1 Gather together a selection of snowdrop bulbs.

2 Clay pots are a good, practical choice, as their porosity means the bulbs are never in overly wet compost. Cover the hole in the base of each pot with a pebble to keep the compost inside and pour in a generous layer of horticultural grit.

3 Partially fill each clay pot with equal measures of compost and grit, to create a beautifully open mix.

4 Take each snowdrop out of its original container, pushing it from the underside to ease it loose and keeping as much of the soil around the roots as possible.

5 Plant one snowdrop in each clay pot to the same depth it was in its original container.

6 Use your fingers to push a little more compost around the sides to fill any gaps.

7 Water carefully to settle the soil around the roots and position the pots where they will avoid excessive winter wet.

Note: Reclamation yards and secondhand shops are a good source of clay pots.

1

Galanthus nivalis 'Anna Mill'
snowdrop

Triangular flowers with straight, narrow petals. Small green spots on inner petals.

bulb
height 20cm (8in)
1 per pot
flowers from mid-winter to late winter

2

Galanthus plicatus 'Bryan Hewitt'
snowdrop

Rounded petals that are nipped at their tips, making them balloon out.

bulb
height 20cm (8in)
1 per pot
flowers from mid-winter to late winter

3

Galanthus plicatus 'Joe Sharman'
snowdrop

The pale petals have green stripes and are bright green inside.

bulb
height 20cm (8in)
1 per pot
flowers from mid-winter to late winter

5

Galanthus woronowii
'Elizabeth Harrison'
snowdrop

Chunkier leaves and faint yellow marks
on each white inner petal.

bulb
height 20cm (8in)
1 per pot
flowers from mid-winter to late winter

Good for...

early bumblebee queens

4

Galanthus plicatus 'Sarah Dumont'
snowdrop

Stooping flowers with unusual, citrus-
yellow markings.

bulb
height 20cm (8in)
1 per pot
flowers from mid-winter to late winter

Grow5 basics

1

Soil

Soil is an ecosystem made up of sand, silt and clay in differing amounts and organic matter from rotting leaves. It can be thin and 'scratchy' or even rubble-filled if building work has taken place, struggling to hold on to moisture, or heavy and compacted, meaning it will be full of water in winter and baked hard and dry in summer.

Before planting, all soils benefit from being dug and the addition of a bag or two of peat-free organic compost to encourage worms and useful fungi, bacteria and microorganisms, all of which are beneficial to plants. Taking care not to step on the soil as you work, tip the compost straight from the bag onto the soil and turn over the compost and the soil with your spade to loosely fold them together.

2

Compost

Plants in containers are completely reliant on what you provide for them, including the compost. There are a number of different composts available. A peat-free, general-purpose compost is suitable for most purposes, but specialist composts (for seed sowing, for example) are also available.

The main differences between one type of compost and another are the nutrients they contain and the sharpness of their drainage. A woody rosemary shrub from the Mediterranean, for instance, likes a scratchy soil and few nutrients, so it's a good idea to add a few scoops of horticultural grit to the potting mix, whereas a fern from the forest floor favours a good depth of dark, damp, humus-rich soil.

3

Watering

It can be beneficial to water plants in their original pots before you plant them. Then water them again to settle the soil around their roots. But routine daily watering of your garden shouldn't be taken as a given. Although all plants need a thorough drench when first planted and regular watering while they settle in, a plant in the open garden that is well-matched to its spot will be able to sustain itself. Always water the soil and not the leaves and flowers. Plants in containers do need to be watered regularly, especially in the height of summer. Always water the compost and not the leaves and flowers, thoroughly drenching it each time. Ideally, water in the cool of the morning or evening.

4

Bulbs

Spring-flowering bulbs have to be planted in the preceding autumn to spend the winter underground in the cold and dark. The darkness and low temperatures allow the flower bud to develop inside the bulb and stimulate gibberellin, the hormone that pulls the flowers up towards the light in springtime. Summer-flowering bulbs, such as lilies, are planted in late winter.

Growing bulbs from scratch rather than buying pots of budding bulbs in spring means you don't have to rely on what commercial growers have selected to offer that year and so offers a much wider choice of flowers. It is also much more economical. As well as planting bulbs outside, I often plant a few in small, individual pots in autumn to transplant into containers later.

5

Annuals, biennials and perennials

annual
A plant that completes its lifecycle in one year.

germination - shoot - flower - seed pod

biennial
A plant that completes its lifecycle in two years.

stems and leaves in year one, then flowers in the second year

perennial
A plant that repeats its flowering cycle year after year.

shoots in spring - flowers in summer - and often architectural seedheads in winter

6

UK seasons

mid-winter	January
late winter	February
early spring	March
mid-spring	April
late spring	May
early summer	June
mid-summer	July
late summer	August
early autumn	September
mid-autumn	October
late autumn	November
early winter	December

7

Making holes in containers

Most containers already have a drainage hole, or holes, in the base, especially those made from clay, terracotta or stone. However, if you are using recycled containers, such as galvanized metal tubs or wooden crates, you may have to add some holes. This is easy to do, either with an electric drill or using a hammer and strong nail. Be sure to wear safety goggles to protect your eyes when making holes in this way. Cover each hole with a pebble to keep the compost inside the container.

8

Botanical names

The botanical name of a plant can feel challenging at first, but using a Latin rather than a common name is the only way you can be sure that the plant you are looking at in the nursery or online is the plant you want and have planned to buy. While many plants share the same common name, a botanical name is unique to each plant. The botanical names of plants are typically comprised of three words: the genus (italicized), the species (also italicized) and the cultivar name (which usually appears in single quotation marks).

The first name, the genus, refers to all the plants in a wide but similar group. For example, all sunflowers are named *Helianthus*. The species name refers to similar plants within that group. So, *Helianthus annuus* are all annual sunflowers. The cultivar name is thought up by the breeder and refers to one specific plant. For instance, *Helianthus annuus* 'Claret' is a plum-coloured, annual sunflower. So, botanical names are very useful, not only helping to identify plants, but also telling us more about them.

Occasionally, plants have an additional part to their name to denote that they have been registered with Plant Breeders' Rights. These are presented differently to other names. For example, in this book, we feature *Pulmonaria* Opal ('Ocupol').

9

Sourcing plants

I prefer buying plants from independent nurseries and online. A trip to an independent nursery is an inspiring way to spend an afternoon and the plants are likely to have been grown by the people who are selling them and they are usually a good source of helpful information and advice. Most nurseries will also put plants aside for collection if you email or telephone ahead with your list.

Recently, ordering online has become one of my favoured ways to buy plants. It offers a huge choice as well as the opportunity to go on a waiting list if the plants I want are out of stock. There is enormous pleasure to be had in pulling the tape from a box of plants delivered to the door. All of the nurseries I have recommended deliver in sustainable packaging.

Traditional garden centres and superstores typically only sell plants that are in flower and tend to have quite a limited selection if you are looking for a specific plant.

Favourite suppliers

Plants and seeds

Beth Chatto's Plants & Gardens
A good selection of perennials, expertly grown.

bethchatto.co.uk

Crocus
The designers' favourite nursery. Crocus grow the plants for the top designers at the RHS Chelsea Flower Show.

crocus.co.uk

Great Dixter House & Gardens
Offers notable seeds and plants, all from the garden's stock, chosen by staff and students.

greatdixter.co.uk

Sarah Raven's Kitchen and Garden
Annual seeds and plug plants, perennials and a choice selection of bulbs.

sarahraven.com

Special Plants

A small but expertly curated selection. Be assured, all the plants offered are good ones.

specialplants.net

Chiltern Seeds
Has the widest range of seeds available. Seeds only.

chilternseeds.co.uk

Bulbs

Avon Bulbs
Bulbs, corms and tubers. Order at any time and they will deliver to you at the correct time of year to plant your bulbs outside.

avonbulbs.co.uk

Peter Nyssen
A good selection of bulbs, all neonicotinoid-free.

peternyssen.com

Organic Bulbs
A carefully curated collection from top planting designers Urquhart & Hunt. Organic.

organicbulbs.com

Compost

Dalefoot Composts
Good-quality, peat-free composts, mostly wool-based, including for seed sowing and general use. Soil Association approved.

dalefootcomposts.co.uk

Melcourt SylvaGrow
Peat-free, organic and made up of a blend of bark, coir and nutrients.

melcourt.co.uk

US suppliers

Floret Flowers
A choice selection of annual flower seeds.

floretflowers.com

Northwind Perennial Farm
Offers notable perennial plants for sale online and for collection in Wisconsin.

northwindperennialfarm.com

Van Engelen
A good selection of bulbs, corms and tubers.

vanenelen.com

Flowering calendar

Spring

Allium tripedale
Allium 'Miami'
Anemone blanda
Crocus 'Ruby Giant'
Dodecatheon jeffreyi
Epimedium pinnatum subsp.
  colchicum
Euphorbia griffithii 'Dixter'

Fritillaria meleagris
Fritillaria michailovskyi
Galanthus nivalis
Lilium martagon
Muscari armeniacum
Narcissus species
Polygonatum x hybridum
Polystichum species
Pulmonaria OPAL ('Ocupol')

Saxifraga × arendsii 'Buttercream'
Sesleria autumnalis
Scilla siberica
Tulipa species
Veronica umbrosa 'Georgia Blue'
Viola labradorica

Early summer

Achillea 'Coronation Gold'
Agrostemma githago 'Alba'
Alchemilla mollis
Allium atropurpureum
Allium christophii
Allium siculum
Allium 'Summer Drummer'
Aloe aristata
Ammi majus
Aquilegia vulgaris 'Munstead White'
Astrantia major 'Large White'
Astrantia 'Roma'
Cenolophium denudatum
Centranthus ruber 'Albus'
Chaerophyllum hirsutum 'Roseum'
Cirsium heterophyllum
Cirsium rivulare 'Atropurpureum'
Digitalis isabelliana BELLA
Digitalis lutea

Digitalis purpurea
Echeveria elegans
Echinops ritro 'Veitch's Blue'
Eryngium × zabelii 'Big Blue'
Fagopyrum dibotrys
Foeniculum vulgare
Galtonia candicans
Geranium 'Orion'
Hakonechloa macra
Hesperis matronalis var. albiflora
Hylotelephium 'Matrona'
Iris 'Italic Light'
Iris 'Sable'
Knautia macedonica
Lobelia × speciosa 'Tania'
Lychnis flos-cuculi 'Nana'
Melica altissima 'Alba'
Orlaya grandiflora
Papaver commutatum 'Ladybird'
Papaver rhoeas
Perovskia atriplicifolia 'Blue Spire'

Phlomis tuberosa 'Amazone'
Pimpinella major 'Rosea'
Polemonium caeruleum
Rudbeckia occidentalis
Salvia argentea 'Artemis'
Salvia nemorosa 'Caradonna'
Salvia officinalis
Salvia × sylvestris 'Rose Queen'
Sambucus nigra 'Black Beauty'
Sanguisorba menziesii
Sedum 'Silver Roses'
Sempervivum calcareum
Sesleria autumnalis
Stipa gigantea
Thalictrum delavayi 'Album'
Tulbaghia violacea
Tulbaghia 'John May's Special'
Verbena bonariensis
Verbena officinalis var. grandiflora
  'Bampton'

Late Summer

Achillea filipendulina 'Gold Plate'
Actaea simplex Atropurpurea
   Group 'James Compton'
Agastache rugosa 'Liquorice Blue'
Alcea rosea 'Giant Single Mixed'
Allium sphaerocephalon
Allium stipitatum ' Mount Everest'
Aloe aristata
Aloysia citrodora
Ammi majus
Atriplex hortensis var. rubra
Briza media
Campanula lactiflora
Cosmos bipinnatus 'Xsenia'
Crocus species
Dahlia species
Deschampsia cespitosa 'Goldtau'
Dianthus superbus

Dianthus barbatus 'Sweet
   Cherry Black'
Digitalis parviflora
Echeveria elegans
Echinacea pallida
Erigeron annuus
Erigeron karvinskianus
Eryngium species
Euphorbia seguieriana
Foeniculum vulgare 'Purpureum'
Liatris pycnostachya
Lilium 'Stracciatella Event'
Linaria vulgaris 'Alba'
Nepeta racemosa 'Walker's Low'
Ocimum basilicum 'Mrs Burns'
   Lemon'
Oenothera biennis
Origanum laevigatum
   'Herrenhausen'
Orlaya grandiflora

Pelargonium species
Perovskia atriplicifolia 'Blue Spire'
Phlomis russeliana
Phlox drummondii 'Cherry Caramel'
Ranunculus acris
Rosmarinus officinalis
   'Miss Jessopp's Upright'
Salvia nemorosa 'Caradonna'
Salvia officinalis
Salvia patens 'Giant Form'
Salvia 'Trewithen Cerise'
Sedum 'Silver Roses'
Sempervivum calcareum
Sempervivum 'Gulle Dame'
Stipa tenuissima
Trachelospermum jasminoides
Verbena bonariensis
Xerochrysum bracteatum
   'Dragon Fire'

Autumn

Actaea simplex Atropurpurea
   Group 'James Compton'
Actaea simplex 'Pink Spike'
Agastache 'Blue Boa'
Alchemilla mollis
Anemanthele lessoniana
Anemone WILD SWAN ('Macane001')
Astrantia major 'Large White'
Dianthus carthusianorum

Digiplexis 'Falcon Fire'
Echinacea purpurea 'White Swan'
Echinacea pallida
Eryngium yuccifolium
Euphorbia corollata
Hydrangea quercifolia
Liatrus spicata
Miscanthus sinensis 'Morning Light'
Molinia caerulea subsp. caerulea
   'Poul Petersen'
Persicaria amplexicaulis 'Alba'

Rosa glauca
Rudbeckia fulgida var. sullivantii
   'Goldsturm'
Salvia 'Amistad'
Sanguisorba officinalis
   'Red Buttons'
Sesleria autumnalis
Symphyotrichum turbinellum
Tulbaghia 'Fairy Star'
Tulbaghia violacea
Verbena bonariensis

Winter

Cyclamen hederifolium
Echinacea purpurea 'White Swan'
Erica × darleyensis

Foeniculum vulgare
Galanthus nivalis
Galanthus plicatus
Galanthus woronowii 'Elizabeth
   Harrison'

Helleborus × sahinii 'Winterbells'
Miscanthus sinensis
Pennisetum alopecuroides
   'Cassian's Choice'
Phlomis russeliana

Index

Index

Author's acknowledgements
A huge thank you to Alison Starling for championing *Grow5* and for careful guidance throughout.

Thank you to Jonathan Christie, David Hawkins, Sybella Stephens and Caroline West at Octopus.

To Jason Ingram, my favourite photographer.

To Hauser and Wirth, Somerset, Hepworth Wakefield, Tom Stuart-Smith, Katy Merrington, Artisan Landscapes, Katie Guillebaud, Andy Sturgeon, Tom Coward, Gravetye Manor, Matthew Reese Malverleys garden, The Cottage Herbery, Keith Wiley at Wildside, Mary Keen, June Blake at June Blake's Garden and Jimi Blake at Hunting Brook.

To Anne, Bill and Victoria.

Picture credits
Photography by Jason Ingram, except page 28 centre: 1319341: Martin Hughes-Jones/ GAP Photos; page 72 right TAGBRG: Gina Kelly/Alamy Stock Photo; page 164 centre Rub003: Andrea Jones/ Garden Exposures Photo Library.

First published in Great Britain in 2022 by Mitchell Beazley, an imprint of Octopus Publishing Group Ltd,
Carmelite House,
50 Victoria Embankment,
London EC4Y 0DZ
www.octopusbooks.co.uk

An Hachette UK Company
www.hachette.co.uk

Text copyright
© Lucy Bellamy 2022
Photography copyright
© Jason Ingram 2022
(except pages 28 centre, 72 right, 164 centre)
Layout and design copyright
© Octopus Publishing Group 2022

Distributed in the US by Hachette Book Group,
1290 Avenue of the Americas,
4th and 5th Floors,
New York, NY 10104

Distributed in Canada by Canadian Manda Group,
664 Annette St.,
Toronto, Ontario,
Canada M6S 2C8

ISBN 978 178472 761 1

A CIP catalogue record for this book is available from the British Library.

Printed and bound in China

10 9 8 7 6 5 4 3 2 1

Publisher:
Alison Starling
Creative Director:
Jonathan Christie
Photographer:
Jason Ingram
Book Design:
Untitled
Senior Managing Editor:
Sybella Stephens
Copy Editor:
Caroline West
Production Manager:
Caroline Alberti